D1634069

# THE UNCYCLOPEDIA

# THE UNCYCLOPEDIA

## Gideon Haigh

TEXT PUBLISHING
MELBOURNE AUSTRALIA

With grateful thanks for the contributions of John Clarke, Philippa Hawker, David Studham, Andrew Turner, Melanie Ostell, George Thomas and Sally Warhaft. *Homines dum docent discunt.*

The Text Publishing Company
171 La Trobe Street
Melbourne Victoria 3000
Australia
www.textpublishing.com.au

All rights reserved. Without limiting the rights under copyright above, no part of this publication shall be reproduced, stored in or introduced into a retrieval system, or transmitted in any form or by any means (electronic, mechanical, photocopying, recording or otherwise), without the prior permission of both the copyright owner and the publisher of this book.

Designed by Peter Long
Typeset in ACaslon by J & M Typesetting
Printed and bound by Griffin Press

National Library of Australia
Cataloguing-in-Publication data:

Haigh, Gideon.
The uncyclopedia.

ISBN 1 877008 87 7.

1. Curiosities and wonders - Australia. 2. Australia - Miscellanea. I. Title.

994

# THE UNCYCLOPEDIA

An epigraph is the superscription of a book appearing near the title page, usually taking the form of an allusive citation hinting to its intent…

> SAMPLE: 'He was dull in a new way, and that made many people think him great.' Samuel Johnson (of Gray)

…or generally to the life of letters.

> SAMPLE: 'Outside of a dog, a book is man's best friend. Inside of a dog, it's too dark to read.' Groucho Marx

A foreword, derived from the German *vorwort*, is properly a 'word in advance' about the book and/or its creator written by someone other than the author.

> SAMPLE: 'I was delighted to get a letter from Mike Brearley from Australia last winter asking me if I'd be "prepared to write the forward" to his next book. Delighted not only because I could leave the letter lying round to impress people; delighted not just that a former philosophy don could make such a basic spelling mistake; but delighted also because I like the man and found his first book *The Return of the Ashes* the most interesting book on cricket I've read.' John Cleese, *The Ashes Retained* by Mike Brearley and Dudley Doust, 1979.

A preface is likewise an advance word, though generally written by the author, and containing advice about their intentions in writing the book.

> SAMPLE: 'Study these rules and imitate the English. There can only be one result: if you don't succeed in imitating them you become ridiculous; if you do, you become even more ridiculous.' George Mikes, *How to Be an Alien*, 1946.

An introduction is a preliminary statement, again by the author, foreshadowing and explaining the book's contents and structure.

SAMPLE: 'Last of all I print the sad letter I received from an unknown lady, written the day before she committed suicide—prompted in part, as it would appear, by gloom engendered by reading my articles in *Spectator*. I hope this book does not have the same effect on many people.' Auberon Waugh, *Another Voice: An Alternative Anatomy of Britain*, 1986.

Acknowledgments may appear at the beginnings or ends of books, to express thanks for specific gestures of assistance or general acts of support and friendship.

SAMPLE: 'Writers often thank their colleagues for their help. Mine have given none...Writers often thank their typists. I thank mine. Mrs George Cook is not a particularly good typist, but her spelling and grammar are good. The responsibility for any mistakes is mine, but the fault is hers. Finally, writers often thank their wives. I have no wife.' Edward Ingram, *The Beginning of the Great Game in Asia 1828–1834*, 1979.

## STAGES OF SLEEP

Human sleep divides into four stages of non-rapid eye movement sleep (NREM) and one of rapid eye movement sleep (REM), occurring in a ninety-minute cycle repeated around five times a night. Cycles gradually replace Stage 3 and 4 sleep with longer periods of alternating Stage 2 and 5 sleep: roughly half the final cycle is Stage 2, half Stage 5. The stages and the portions they represent of a normal night's sleep are as follows:

*Stage 1:* Transitional sleep, 2–5 per cent.

*Stage 2:* Baseline sleep, 45–60 per cent: brainwaves follow 'theta' rhythms.

*Stage 3 and 4:* Slow Wave sleep, 30–40 per cent: brainwaves follow slower 'delta' rhythms. This is the deepest and most restorative form of sleep.

*Stage 5:* REM sleep, 20–25 per cent: breathing, heart rate and brain wave activity quicken. Dreams occur.

## THIRTY SONGS CONTAINING RADIO
## IN THE TITLE

———•◦•———

'Biological Radio' . . . . . . . . . . . . . . . . . . . . . . . . . Dreadzone, 2001
'Capital Radio' . . . . . . . . . . . . . . . . . . . . . . . . . . . The Clash, 1981
'Do You Remember Rock'n'Roll Radio?' . . . . . The Ramones, 1980
'I Bet You They Won't Play This Song on the Radio' . . . . . . . . . . .
                                                    Monty Python, 1980
'Life Is a Rock, But the Radio Rolled Me' . . . Tracey Ullman, 1992
'Mexican Radio' . . . . . . . . . . . . . . . . . . . . . . . Wall of Voodoo, 1983
'On My Radio'. . . . . . . . . . . . . . . . . . . . . . . . . . The Selecter, 1979
'On the Radio'. . . . . . . . . . . . . . . . . . . . . . . . . . . Cheap Trick, 1978
'Radio Africa'. . . . . . . . . . . . . . . . . . . . . . . . . Latin Quarter, 1982
'Radio and TV' . . . . . . . . . . . . . . . . . . . . . . . . . Kris Jensen, 1962
'Radio Clash' . . . . . . . . . . . . . . . . . . . . . . . . . . . . The Clash, 1981
'Radio Cure' . . . . . . . . . . . . . . . . . . . . . . . . . . . . . . Wilco, 2002
'Radio Ethiopia/Abyssinia'. . . . . . . . . . . . . . . . . . Patti Smith, 1976
'Radio Four'. . . . . . . . . . . . . . . . . . . . : Public Image Limited, 1979
'Radio 55' . . . . . . . . . . . . . . . . . . . . . . . . . . . . Teengenerate, 1995
'Radio Free Europe' . . . . . . . . . . . . . . . . . . . . . . . . . REM, 1981
'Radio Gaga'. . . . . . . . . . . . . . . . . . . . . . . . . . . . . . Queen, 1984
'Radio, Jukebox and TV' . . . . . . . . . . . . . . . . . Jimmy Donley, 1958
'Radio On'. . . . . . . . . . . . . . . . . . . . . . . . . Kissing the Pink, 1984
'Radio Radio'. . . . . . . . . . . . . . . . . . . . . . . . Elvis Costello, 1977
'Radio Silence'. . . . . . . . . . . . . . . . . . . . . . . . . . . Blue Peter, 1984
'Radio Silence'. . . . . . . . . . . . . . . . . . . . . . . . Elvis Costello, 2002
'Radio Silence' . . . . . . . . . . . . . . . . . . . . . . . Thomas Dolby, 1982
'Radio Song'. . . . . . . . . . . . . . . . . . . . . . . . . . . . . . . REM, 1991
'Radio Sweetheart'. . . . . . . . . . . . . . . . . . . . . Elvis Costello, 1979
'The Radio Story'. . . . . . . . . . . . . . . . . . . . . Alternative TV, 1978
'Touch the Radio' . . . . . . . . . . . . . . . . . . . . Dance Language, 1983
'Turn Your Radio On'. . . . . . . . . . . . . . . . . . . . Ray Turner, 1972
'Video Killed the Radio Star'. . . . . . . . . . . . . . The Buggles, 1979
'Who Listens to the Radio?'. . . . . . . . . . . . . . . . The Sports, 1979

*A mari usque ad mare* (L: From sea to sea)
Canada, derived from Psalm 72:8:
'He shall have dominion from sea to sea.'

*Ac majorem Dei gloriam* (L: To the Greater Glory of God)
The Jesuits, Roman Catholic religious order founded by
St Ignatius Loyola (c. 1491–1556) in 1534.

*Aut Caesar, aut nihil* (L: Caesar or nothing)
Inscribed on the sword of Cesare Borgia (1476–1507).

*Bene qui sedulo* (L: He lives well who lives industriously)
Lords Northcliffe (1865–1922) and Rothermere (1925–1998),
British press barons.

*Candor illaesus* (L: Purity unsullied)
Giulio de Medici (1478–1534), nephew of Lorenzo the
Magnificent, Pope Clement VII from 1523.

*Cedo nuli* (L: I yield to none)
Desiderius Erasmus (c. 1466–1536), Dutch humanist and theologian.

*Christus vincit, Christus regnat, Christus triumphat*
(L: Christ conquers, Christ reigns, Christ triumphs)
Charlemagne (742–814), Emperor of the West.

*Cum grege non graditur* (L: He does not walk with the flock)
Cardinal Benedetti Odescalchi (1611–1689),
Pope Innocent XI from 1676.

*Dieu et mon droit* (Fr: God and my right)
English and British sovereigns, coined in 1198 by
Richard I (1157–1199) after his victory at Gisors.

*E pluribus unum* (L: From the many, one)
United States of America, adopted in 1782; the 'many' refers
to the thirteen original colonies, the 'one' to their union.

*Exemplum adest ipse homo*
(L: The man himself is present as an example)
The Franklin family of the USA, including Benjamin (1706–1790).

*Felis demulcta mitis* (L: A stroked cat is gentle)
The Lords Brocket, British aristocrats, lately disgraced by
conviction of present Lord in insurance scam. According to
Tony Blair, in February 1997: 'The first Lord Brocket bought the
title from Lloyd George; the second Lord Brocket was one of
Britain's leading Nazi sympathisers; and the third Lord Brocket is
serving five years for fraud.'

*Fiat justitia et pereas mundus*
(L: Let justice be done, though the world perish)
Ferdinand I (1503–1564), Holy Roman Emperor.

*Hoc pretium cive servato tulit*
(L: He bears this reward for having saved a citizen)
Appears on the Medal of the Royal Humane Society.

*Honi soit qui mal y pense* (F: Evil be to him who evil thinks)
Order of the Garter, founded by Edward III in 1348.

*Ich dien* (Ger: I serve)
The Prince of Wales.

*Invidiae fines virtute reliquit*
(L: He left the bounds of envy by valour)
Jules Mazarin (1602–1661), French statesman and cardinal.

*Nation shall speak unto nation*
The British Broadcasting Corporation, adapted from Micah 4:3:
'Nation shall not lift up a sword against nation.'

*Praestat uni probo qum mille improbis placere*
(L: Better I should please one good man than a thousand bad men)
Friedrich I (c. 1122–1190), Holy Roman Emperor and
German king.

*Unus non sufficit orbis* (L: One world is not enough)
Philip II (1527–1598), King of Spain.

*Ventis secundus* (L: By favourable winds)
HMS *Hood* (1918–1941), British battlecruiser, sunk in
engagement with the *Bismarck* in Denmark Strait.

John Adrian Louis Hope, 7th Earl of Hopetoun †
1 January 1901 – 9 January 1903

Hallam Tennyson, 2nd Baron Tennyson
9 January 1903 – 21 January 1904

Henry Stafford Northcote, 1st Baron Northcote
21 January 1904 – 9 September 1908

William Humble Ward, 2nd Earl of Dudley
9 September 1908 – 3 July 1911

Thomas Denman, 3rd Baron Denman
3 July 1911 – 18 May 1914

Sir Ronald Craufurd Munro-Ferguson
18 May 1914 – 6 October 1920

Henry William Forster, 1st Baron Forster
6 October 1920 – 8 October 1925

John Lawrence Baird, 1st Baron Stonehaven
8 October 1925 – 22 January 1931

Sir Isaac Alfred Isaacs ^
22 January 1931 – 23 January 1936

Brigadier-General Alexander Gore Arkwright Hore-Ruthven,
1st Baron Gowrie
23 January 1936 – 30 January 1945

HRH Prince Henry William Frederick Albert, Duke of Gloucester,
Earl of Ulster and Baron Culloden
30 January 1945 – 11 March 1947

Sir William John McKell ^
11 March 1947 – 8 May 1953

Field-Marshal Sir William Joseph Slim
8 May 1953 – 2 February 1960

William Shepherd Morrison, 1st Viscount Dunrossil *
2 February 1960 – 3 February 1961

William Philip Sidney, 1st Viscount de L'Isle
3 August 1961 – 22 September 1965

Richard Gardiner Casey, Baron Casey ^
22 September 1965 – 30 April 1969

Sir Paul Meernaa Caedwalla Hasluck ^
30 April 1969 – 11 July 1974

Sir John Robert Kerr ^ †
11 July 1974 – 8 December 1977

Sir Zelman Cowen ^
8 December 1977 – 29 July 1982

Sir Ninian Martin Stephen ^
29 July 1982 – 15 February 1989

William George Hayden ^
16 February 1989 – 15 February 1996

Sir William Patrick Deane ^
16 February 1996 – 28 June 2001

Archbishop Peter John Hollingworth ^ †
29 June 2001 – 29 May 2003

Major-General Michael Jeffrey ^
11 August 2003 –

---

^ Australian   * Died in office   † Resigned prematurely

The five sons of Minnie and Sam Marx: 'Groucho' (Julius; 1890–1977); 'Chico' (Leonard; 1891–1961); 'Gummo' (Milton; 1892–1977), 'Harpo' (Arthur; 1893–1964); 'Zeppo' (Herbert; 1901–1979). Groucho, Chico and Harpo appeared in thirteen films: *The Cocoanuts*, 1929; *Animal Crackers*, 1930; *Monkey Business*, 1931; *Horse Feathers*, 1932; *Duck Soup*, 1933; *A Night at the Opera*, 1935; *A Day at the Races*, 1937; *Room Service*, 1938; *At the Circus*, 1939; *Go West*, 1940; *The Big Store*, 1941; *A Night in Casablanca*, 1946; *The Story of Mankind*, 1957 (Marx brothers do not appear together). Zeppo did not appear in movies after 1935; Gummo not at all.

## TWELVE MEN TO WALK ON THE MOON

The three-man circumlunar Apollo program set as a national goal by President John F. Kennedy in May 1961 originally encompassed twenty missions. Apollos 1–6 were test flights of the Saturn 1 and Saturn 5 boosters from May 1964 to April 1968. Apollos 7–10 were increasingly ambitious manned flights between October 1968 and May 1969: Apollo 11 fulfilled Kennedy's *fiat* after expenditure of $US24 billion. Because Apollo 13 was aborted in April 1970 when a malfunctioning fuel cell exploded, and Apollos 18–20 were cancelled because of budgetary restraints, only a dozen Americans—including a single civilian—have trodden the lunar surface.

NEIL ARMSTRONG (US NAVY); EDWIN ALDRIN (US AIR FORCE)
Apollo 11's lunar module *Eagle* landed in the Sea of Tranquillity on 21 July 1969, 6.5 kilometres from its target point. Armstrong was first on the moon because the module's forward hatch hinged on the right. The plaque attached to their 1.52-metre-high American flag reads: 'Here men from the planet Earth first set foot upon the Moon, July 1969 AD. We came in peace for all mankind.'

CHARLES CONRAD (US NAVY); ALAN BEAN (US NAVY)
Apollo 12's lunar module *Intrepid* landed in the Ocean of Storms on 18 November 1969, only 183 metres from the unmanned *Surveyor 3*, which soft-landed thirty-one months earlier. Conrad and Bean spent 31.5 hours on the moon, including 7.5 in two moon walks, collecting 34 kilograms of samples.

ALAN SHEPARD (US NAVY); EDGAR MITCHELL (US NAVY)
Apollo 14's lunar module *Antares* landed at Fra Mauro in the Sea of Rains on 5 February 1971. Forty-seven-year-old Shepard, the first American in space almost a decade earlier, also became the first man to play golf on the moon, using two balls he had smuggled aboard and a pole from a solar wind experiment.

DAVID SCOTT (US AIR FORCE); JAMES IRWIN (US AIR FORCE)
Apollo 15's lunar module *Falcon* landed at Hadley Rille on 30 July 1971, carrying the first motor vehicle on the moon, the Boeing-designed Lunar Rover. Its TV camera filmed their departure for the first time.

JOHN YOUNG (US NAVY); CHARLES DUKE (US AIR FORCE)
Apollo 16's lunar module *Orion* landed at Descartes on 21 April 1972, avoiding a 7.6-metre-deep crater by only three metres. Young, who had earlier orbited the moon on Apollo 10, became the only man to do so twice.

EUGENE CERNAN (US NAVY); HARRISON SCHMITT (CIVILIAN GEOLOGIST)
Apollo 17's lunar module *Challenger* landed at Taurus-Littrow on 11 December 1972. This was the longest Apollo flight (301 hours 52 minutes), spent the most time on the lunar surface (22 hours 6 minutes), and involved the biggest retrieval (113 kg of samples).

FOUR HORSEMEN OF THE APOCALYPSE

WAR – White horse — SLAUGHTER – Red Horse —
FAMINE – Black Horse — DEATH – Pale Horse

*Inches (millimetres) per hour/Condition*

0.002 (0.0508) mist; 0.005 (0.127) fog; 0.01 (0.254) drizzle; 0.04 (1.016) light rain; 0.15 (3.81) moderate rain; 0.6 (15.24) heavy rain; 1.6 (40.64) excessive rain; 4.0 (101.6) cloudburst.

## AUSTRALIAN ANTARCTIC TERRITORY

Since an imperial order in June 1933 settling Britain's possession on Australia, this country has laid claim to 42 per cent of Antarctica. The Australian Antarctic Territory extends from 45° East to 160° East—excluding a section between 136° East and 142° East claimed by France—and includes all islands south of the 60 degree parallel. In December 1947, Macquarie Station, Heard and MacDonald islands were officially added to the territory and made the responsibility of Australian Antarctic Division. The area's population, centred for the last half-century on AAD's Mawson station, varies between 200 in summer and seventy-five in winter. The region also includes the highest points on Australian soil: Mount McClintock, in the eastern sector, rises 3490 metres; Mount Menzies, in the western sector, rises 3355 metres. The grant of the land has not been recognised by the United Nations.

## TYPES OF ADZE

American—Brazilian Slot—Carver's—Chairmaker's Howel—Cleaving—Cooper's Chimney-Pipe—Cooper's Trussing—Fruit—Herring Barrel —Guttering—Joiner's Norfolk—Lipped Ladle—Platelayer's—Saddle-Tree Maker's—Saint Michael's—Shipwright's—Spoonmaker's— Spout—Stirrup—Timber Rafting—Trackmen's Spiking—Trimming— Turkish—Wheelwright's

Harris—George—J
*based, respectively, on:*
Carl Hentschel—George Wingrave—Jerome K. Jerome

## NAMING OF DINOSAURS

The extinct reptiles defined as *dinosauria* were first grouped by Sir Richard Owen, commissioned in 1838 by the British Association for the Advancement of Science to examine the country's fossils. He believed initially that he was studying outsized lizards, but certain physical characteristics common to Iguanodon, Megalosaurus and Hylaeosaurus not shared with modern reptiles convinced him that they deserved a separate recognition; the designation he chose for his April 1842 report combined the Greek *deinos* (fearfully great) and *sauros* (lizard).

The right to name a new genus or species of dinosaur remains the preserve of its discoverer, subject to approval by the International Commission on Zoological Nomenclature. The names are usually derived from some unusual feature of the creature, sometimes for its imagined behaviour, occasionally for its place of discovery, and intermittently in honour of a person.

### Dinosaurs named for head features

| | |
|---|---|
| Corythosaurus | Helmet lizard |
| Dilophosaurus | Two-ridged lizard |
| Ornatotholus | Ornate dome |
| Pachyrhinosaurus | Thick-nosed Lizard |
| Pentaceratops | Five-horned head |
| Saurolophus | Crested lizard |
| Triceratops | Three-horned head |

### Dinosaurs named for body features

| | |
|---|---|
| Baryonyx | Heavy claw |
| Dacentrus | Sharp-point tail |
| Deinocheirus | Terrible hand |
| Elaphrosaurus | Lightweight lizard |
| Panoplosaurus | Fully-armed lizard |

### Dinosaurs named for teeth

| | |
|---|---|
| Astrodon | Star tooth |
| Deinodon | Terrible tooth |
| Heterodontosaurus | Different-tooth lizard |
| Hypsilophodon | High-ridged tooth |
| Iguanodon | Iguana tooth |

### Dinosaurs named for feet

| | |
|---|---|
| Brachypodosaurus | Short-footed lizard |
| Deinonychus | Terrible claw |
| Saltopus | Leaping foot |
| Velocipes | Swift foot |

### Dinosaurs named for imagined behaviour

| | |
|---|---|
| Maiasaura | Good mother lizard |
| Oviraptor | Egg thief |
| Velociraptor | Speedy robber |

### Dinosaurs named for places

| | |
|---|---|
| Albertosaurus | Alberta, Canada |
| Andesaurus | The Andes |
| Denversaurus | Denver, Colorado, USA |
| Lesothosaurus | Lesotho |
| Muttaburrasaurus | Muttaburra, Qld, Australia |
| Utahraptor | Utah, USA |

### Dinosaurs named for paleontologists

| | |
|---|---|
| Chassternbergia | Charles Sternberg |
| Lambeosaurus | Lawrence Lambe |
| Marshosaurus | Othaniel C. Marsh |

| | |
|---|---|
| *AAAP* | American Association of Avian Pathologists. |
| *AUC* | *Ab Urbe Condita.* Latin: from the building of the city, i.e. Rome. |
| *BOVRIL* | *Bo*: Latin for ox; *Vril*: electromagnetic life force in Edward Bulwer-Lytton's sf novel *The Coming Race* (1871). The name was conceived by Bovril's inventor John Lawson Johnston. |
| *CHAPS* | Clearing House Automated Payment System: British banking settlement system. |
| *CRISP* | Computerised Retrieval of Information from Scientific Projects: US medical database. |
| *DRAMBUIE* | A contraction of the Scottish Gaelic expression *an dram buidheach*, literally 'the drink that satisfies'. |
| *FIASCO* | Fixed Income Annual Sporting Clays Outing: skeet-shooting party for derivatives salesmen at Morgan Stanley, which gave its name to Frank Partnoy's *FIASCO: Blood in the Water on Wall Street* (1997). |
| *FIDE* | *Federation Internationale des Echecs.* French: International Chess Federation. |
| *GULAG* | *Glavnoye Upravleniye Lagerei.* Russian: the State Administration of Labour Camps. |
| *IGADD* | Intergovernmental Authority on Drought and Development: seven-member international body for discussion of drought-related matters, founded in Djibouti in 1986. |
| *INRI* | *Iesus Nazarenes Rex Iudaeorum.* Latin: Jesus of Nazareth, King of the Jews. |
| *KGB* | *Komitet Gosudarstvennoi Bezopasnosti.* Russian: Committee of State Security. |
| *LEGO* | *Leg godt.* Danish: Play well. In Latin, coincidentally, *lego* means 'I am joining together' or 'I am reading'— a fact unknown to inventor Ole Kirk Christiansen. |
| *LLB* | *Legum Bacclaureas.* Latin: Bachelor of Laws. |

| | |
|---|---|
| *LSD* | *Librus, Solidi, Denarii.* Latin: pounds, shillings, pence. |
| *MAFIA* | *Morte Alla Francia Italia Anela.* |
| | Italian: 'Death to the French is Italy's cry'. |
| *MIRV* | Multiple Independently targeted Re-entry Vehicle: guided ballistic missile with more than one warhead. |
| *SMERSH* | *Smert shpionam.* Russian: 'Death to spies'. Counter-espionage division of KGB. |
| *SPECTRE* | Special Executive for Counterintelligence, Terrorism, Revenge and Extortion: fictional crime group led by the mysterious Blofeld in five James Bond novels by Ian Fleming. |
| *SPQR* | *Senatus populusque Romanus.* Latin: 'the Senate and the Roman people'. |
| *STRIPS* | Separate Trading of Registered Interest and Principal of Securities: the practice of separating the corpus and the coupon of a bond and trading them as separate securities. |
| *TALISMAN* | Transfer Account Lodgement for Investors, Stock Management for Market-makers: British equities settlement system. |
| *VELCRO* | Contraction of the French *velours crochet* (hooked velvet), devised by its Swiss inventor, de Mestral. |
| *VIYELLA* | Contraction of Via Gellia, a valley near Matlock Bath, Derbyshire, from where the unshrinkable cloth of cotton and wool originated in the 1890s. |

## THE TWELVE MONTHS

Snowy, Flowy, Blowy,
  Showery, Flowery, Bowery,
    Hoppy, Croppy, Droppy,
      Breezy, Sneezy, Freezy.

*from the poem by George Ellis (1753–1815)*

LANGUAGE, TOAST, MEANING

Czech
*Na zdravi (pron: NAHZ-dráh-vee)*
Health

Dutch
*Proost (pron: prohst)*
May it benefit

French
*À votre santé (pron: ah VOH-truh SAH-tay)*
To your health

Hebrew
*L'chaim*
To life

Hungarian
*Egeszsegedre (pron: eh-geh-SHEE-geh-dreh)*
Health

Irish/Scottish
*Slainthe (pron: SLAHN-cheh)*
Health

Italian
*Alla tua salute (pron: ah-lah TOO-ah sah-LOO-tay)*
To your health

Norwegian/Swedish/Finnish
*Skål (pron: Skohl)*
Cup, bowl

Portuguese
*À sua saúde (pron: ah SOO-ah sah-OO-deh)*
To your health

Spanish
*Salud (pron: sah-LOOD)*
Health

In the novels and short stories of P. G. Wodehouse (1881–1975), the impact of American money and glamour on staid English ways is a recurrent theme. Such wealth is at times personified by a Hollywood movie mogul whose reputation usually precedes him. Herewith a dozen examples:

| Mogul | Motion Picture Company | Work |
|---|---|---|
| Theodore P. Brinkmeyer | Brinkmeyer-Magnifico | *Laughing Gas* (1936) |
| Isidore Fishbein | Perfecto-Fishbein | 'The Rise of Minna Nordstrom' (1933) |
| Sigismund Glutz | Medulla-Oblongata-Glutz | 'The Rise of Minna Nordstrom' (1933) |
| Jacob Glutz | Medulla-Oblongata-Glutz | *The Old Reliable* (1951) |
| Ivor 'Jumbo' Llewelyn | Superba-Llewelyn | *The Luck of the Bodkins* (1935), *Frozen Assets* (1964), *Pearls, Girls and Monty Bodkin* (1972), *Bachelors Anonymous* (1973) |
| Jacob Z. Schnellenhamer | Perfecto-Zizzbaum | 'Monkey Business' (1932), 'The Nodder' (1932) |
| Isadore Zinzinheimer | Bigger, Better and Brighter | *Came the Dawn* (1927) |
| Ben Zizzbaum | Zizzbaum-Celluloid | 'The Rise of Minna Nordstrom' (1933) |

China, Russian Federation 14; Brazil 10; Congo, Germany, Sudan 9; Austria, France, Tanzania, Turkey, Zambia 8.

## SAID OF DON KING

A former racketeer who served four years for manslaughter (1967–70), Don King (b. 1931) began his career as a boxing promoter with Muhammad Ali's comeback bout in 1970, and as the manager of Larry Holmes and Mike Tyson controlled the heavyweight title between 1978 and 1990.

'I'm the best promoter in the world because I haven't taken a day off since I left the penitentiary, and because I've read all the great philosophers like St Thomas Aquinine. I am a true attestation of the American dream.' *Don King*

'I never cease to amaze myself. I say this humbly.' *Don King*

'He treated me like a sucker, but I respect him for it.' *Larry Holmes*

'We all know what Don King is, but if you keep a snake in the room and the light on, you can control him.' *Mike Tyson*

'If you don't follow Don King, you get stepped on.' *Tim Witherspoon*

'Don King is a liar and a thief, the greediest bastard I've ever known. The guy wants all the money and all the fighters. He talks about fairness and equality, but he wants everything for himself. If I was a fighter and needed a promoter, who would I take? Don King. The man is the best. Don King delivers.' *Richie Giachetti*

'Don King is one of the great humanitarians of our time. He has risen above that great term "prejudice". He has screwed everybody he has been around. Hog, frog or dog, it don't matter to Don. If you got a quarter, he wants the first twenty-six cents.' *Tex Cobb*

*Some rules of 'the Best Society' imparted by Emily Post in* Etiquette in Society, in Business, in Politics and at Home *(1922).*

There is a quality of protectiveness in a man's expression as it falls on his betrothed, as though she were so lovely a breath might break her; and in the eyes of a girl whose love is really deep, there is always evidence of that most beautiful look of championship, as though she thought: 'No one else can possibly know how wonderful he is!'

The pretty young woman living alone, must literally follow Cinderella's habits.

No lady should cross her knees so that her skirts go up to or above them; neither should her foot be thrust out so that her toes are at knee level.

In good society ladies do not kiss each other when they meet either at parties or in public.

To the bore life holds no dullness; every subject is of unending delight. A story told for the thousandth time has not lost its thrill; every tiresome detail is held up and turned about as a morsel of delectableness; to him each pea in a pod differs from another with the entrancing variety that artists find in tropical sunsets.

'Tintinnabulary summons', meaning bell, and 'Bovine continuation', meaning cow's tail, are more amusing than offensive, but they illustrate the theory of bad style that is pretentious.

Having risen to go, go! Don't stand and keep your hostess standing while you say good-bye, and make a last remark last half an hour!

### THE SEVEN AGAINST THEBES

Polynices—Adrastus—Capaneus—Tydeus—Parthenopaeus—
Hippomedon—Amphiaraus

The post of Britain's court poet has had some masterful and mediocre occupants, from Wordsworth (though he produced no poetry during his tenancy) to Pye (whose works have been out of print for 180 years). The title arises from the old custom at English universities of presenting laurel wreaths to graduates in rhetoric and versification. It was first associated with John Key, in the reign of Edward IV. Ben Jonson is considered the original poet laureate, from 1616, although John Dryden was the first to be appointed and paid a formal stipend (in his case £200 and a butt of sack); he was also the first and only laureate to be fired, for converting to Catholicism. Inflation and austerity have reduced the fee to a token amount—it was commuted during Southey's tenancy to an annual sum of £27—but Sir John Betjeman suggested and received the reinstatement of a yearly wine allowance from the royal cellar. The following is a list of laureates, with a representative snatch of their verse.

1668 – 1688
John Dryden (1631–1700)
'Bold knaves thrive without one grain of sense/But good men starve for want of impudence.'

1688 – 1692
Thomas Shadwell (1642?–1692)
'Words may be false and full of art/Sighs are the natural language of the heart.'

1692 – 1715
Nahum Tate (1652–1715)
'While shepherds watched their flocks by night/All seated on the ground/The Angel of the Lord came down/And glory shone around.'

1715 – 1718
Nicholas Rowe (1674–1718)
'Like Helen, in the night when Troy was sacked/Spectatress of the mischief which she made.'

1718 – 1730
Laurence Eusden (1688–1730)
'Thy virtues shine particularly nice/Ungloomed with a confinity to vice.'

1730 – 1757
Colley Cibber (1671–1757)
'Oh! how many torments lie in the small circle of a wedding-ring!'

1757 – 1785
William Whitehead (1715–1785)
'The Laureat's odes are sung but once/And then not heard—while your renown/For half a season stuns the town.'

1785 – 1790
Thomas Warton (1728–1790)
'All human race, from China to Peru/Pleasure, howe'er disguis'd by art, pursue.'

1790 – 1813
Henry James Pye (1745–1813)
'Firm are the sons that Britain leads/To combat on the main/And firm her hardy race that treads/In steady march the plain.'

1813 – 1843
Robert Southey (1774–1843)
'And everybody praised the Duke/Who this great fight did win. /"But what good came of it at last?" quoth little Peterkin./"Why that I cannot tell," said he,/ "But 'twas a famous victory."'

1843 – 1850
William Wordsworth (1770–1850)
'Bliss was it in that dawn to be alive/But to be young was very heaven!'

1850 – 1892
Alfred Tennyson (1809–1892)
'My strength is as the strength of ten/Because my heart is pure.'

1896 – 1913
Alfred Austin (1835–1913)
'Across the wires the electric message came/He is not better: he is much the same.'

1913 – 1930
Robert Bridges (1844–1930)
'When men were all asleep the snow came flying/In large white flakes over the city brown.'

1930 – 1967
John Masefield (1878–1967)
'I must go down to the sea again/To the lonely sea and the sky/And all I ask is a tall ship/And a star to sail her by.'

1968 – 1972
Cecil Day-Lewis (1904–1972)
'It is the logic of our times/No subject for immortal verse/That we who lived by honest dreams/Defend the bad against the worse.'

1972 – 1984
John Betjeman (1906–1984)
'Come friendly bombs and fall on Slough/It isn't fit for humans now/There isn't grass to graze a cow/Swarm over, Death!'

1984 – 1998
Ted Hughes (1930–1998)
'Ten years after your death/I meet, on a page of your journal/The shock of your joy.'

1998 –
Andrew Motion (1952–)
'Beside the river, swerving under ground/Your future tracked you, snapping at your heels:/Diana, breathless, hunted by your own quick hounds.'

## MONUMENT TO AN INSECT

Queensland's Boonarga Cactoblastis Memorial, erected in 1936, celebrates the introduction of the *Cactoblastis cactorum* moth from South America ten years earlier. Its larvae eradicated a plague of prickly pear which had rendered 25 million hectares of arable land unusable.

| | |
|---|---|
| *aleuromancy* | by flour or meal |
| *alphitomancy* | by barley meal |
| *anthracomancy* | by burning coal |
| *arithmancy* | by numbers |
| *astragalomancy* | by dice |
| *capnomancy* | by smoke |
| *ceraunoscopy* | by lightning |
| *ceromancy* | by melted wax dropped in water |
| *coscinomancy* | with a sieve suspended on shears |
| *crithomancy* | by cake dough |
| *cromnyomancy* | by onions |
| *enoptromancy* | by a mirror |
| *gastromancy* | by ventriloquism |
| *gyromancy* | by walking in circles until dizzy |
| *ichthyomancy* | by fish offal |
| *knissomancy* | by incense burning |
| *lampadomancy* | by the flame of a torch |
| *lecanomancy* | by looking at water in a basin |
| *meteoromancy* | by the weather |
| *metopomancy* | by examining the face |
| *myomancy* | by studying mice |
| *omphalomancy* | predicting the number of children a woman will bear by counting the knots in her first-born's umbilicus |
| *onimancy* | by studying the person's fingernails |
| *pegomancy* | by studying bubbles in a fountain |
| *psephomancy* | by pebbles |
| *retromancy* | by things seen over one's shoulder |
| *scapulimancy* | by studying charred or cracked shoulder blade |
| *scatomancy* | by studying faeces |
| *spasmatomancy* | by studying twitching body |
| *theriomancy* | by studying wild animals |
| *trochomancy* | by wheel tracks |
| *tyromancy* | by watching cheese coagulate |

## EIGHT MAXIMS OF STRATEGY

*In Chapter 20 of his 1968 classic,* Strategy, *military theorist and historian Sir Basil Liddell-Hart delineated the following eight maxims:*

1 Adjust your end to your means.
2 Keep your object always in mind, while adapting your plan to circumstances.
3 Choose the line (or course) of least expectation.
4 Exploit the line of least resistance—so long as it can lead you to any objective that would contribute to your underlying object.
5 Take a line of operation which offers alternative objectives.
6 Ensure that both plans and dispositions are flexible—adaptable to circumstances.
7 Do not throw your weight into a stroke whilst your opponent is on guard—whilst he is well placed to parry or evade it.
8 Do not renew an attack along the same line (or in the same form) after it has once failed.

## WORLD'S TEN BIGGEST EMPLOYERS

1. Wal-Mart stores (US) 1,300,000; 2. China National Petroleum (PRC) 1,146,194; 3. Sinopec (PRC) 917,100; 4. US Postal Service (US) 854,376; 5. Agricultural Bank of China (PRC) 490,999; 6. Siemens (Germany) 426,000; 7. McDonald's (USA) 413,000; 8. Industrial & Commercial Bank of China (PRC) 405,000; 9. Carrefour (France) 396,662; 10. Compass Group (UK) 392,352.

*figures for Financial Year 2002*

## THE FAMOUS FIVE

Julian—Dick—Anne—George—Timmy (the dog)

1 Course; 1a Studding-sails; 2 Fore-topsail; 2a Studding-sails; 3 Main-topsail; 3a Studding-sails; 4 Mizen-topsail; 4a Studding-sails; 5 Fore-topgallant-sail; 5a Studding-sails; 6 Main-topgallant-sail; 6a Studding-sails; 7 Mizen-topgallant-sail; 8 Fore-royal-topsail; 8a Studding-sails; 9 Main-royal-topsail; 9a Studding-sails; 10 Mizen-royal-topsail; 11 Fore-skysail-topsail; 12 Main-skysail-topsail; 13 Mizen-skysail-topsail; 14 Fore-topmast-skysail jib; 15 Jib; 16 Flying jib; 17 Mizen spanker; 18 Spenser; 19 Main-royal-staysail; 20 Main-topgallant-staysail; 21 Mizen-royal-staysail.

In his seminal book on lying and its detection, *Telling Lies* (1985), psychologist Paul Ekman of the University of California provides useful definitions for aspects of the interpretation of truth and untruth.

| | |
|---|---|
| *Leakage* | When a liar inadvertently reveals the truth. |
| *Deception Clue* | When a liar suggests they are lying without revealing the truth. |
| *Brokaw Hazard* | Misjudging a truthful person who happens to be naturally convoluted in speech. (Named for NBC journalist Tom Brokaw who believed he could detect lies verbally from an interviewee's circumlocution.) |
| *Othello Error* | Misjudging a truthful person by failing to take into account the stress of being disbelieved. (Inspired by the climactic scene in Shakespeare's tragedy where the Moor misinterprets Desdemona's distress as guilt.) |
| *Trojan Horse Strategy* | Where the interlocutor pretends to believe the respondent in the hope the respondent will become entangled in their own fabrications. |

## FABERGÉ EGGS
————•◦•————

Forty-nine of the intricate and valuable gift eggs made by court jeweller Carl Fabergé over thirty years from 1885 for Tsars Aleksandr III and Nikolai II survive. The ten considered of greatest merit and beauty are: the Resurrection Egg, Azova Egg, Renaissance Egg, Caucasus Egg, Danish Palaces Egg, Revolving Miniatures Egg, Coronation Egg, Empress Marie Egg, Lilies of the Valley Egg, Trans-Siberian Egg.

*Allman, Duane (Howard)* (1946–1971). Founder of the Allman Brothers. Rose Hill Cemetery, Macon, Bibb County, Georgia, USA.

*Hendrix, Jimi* (1942–1970). Guitarist The Jimi Hendrix Experience. Greenwood Memorial Park, Renton, King County, Washington, USA.

*Holly, Buddy* (1936–1959). Lead singer The Crickets. City of Lubbock Cemetery, Lubbock, Lubbock County, Texas, USA.

*Hutchence, Michael* (1960–1997). Lead singer INXS. Northern Suburbs Memorial Gardens & Crematorium, Sydney.

*Morrison, Jim* (1943–1971). Lead singer Doors. Le Pere Lachaise, Paris, France.

*Presley, Elvis* (1935–1977). Singer. Graceland Mansion Estates, Memphis, Shelby County, Tennessee, USA.

*Scott, Bon* (1946–1980). Lead singer AC/DC. Fremantle Cemetery, Fremantle.

*Spungen, Nancy* (1958–1978). Sid Vicious' girlfriend (his ashes, allegedly, were scattered on the grave). King David Cemetery, Bensalem, Bucks County, Pennsylvania, USA.

*Thunders, Johnny* (1952–1991). Guitarist New York Dolls/ Heartbreakers. Saint Mary's Cemetery, Flushing, Queens County, New York, USA. Plot: Section 9, Grave R78-82.

*Valens, Ritchie* (1941–1959) Guitarist/Singer. San Fernando Mission Cemetery, Mission Hills, Los Angeles County, California, USA. Plot: Section C, Lot 248, Grave 2.

## SHIPBOARD WATCHES

8 pm–12 am *First*; 12 am–4 am *Middle*; 4 am–8 am *Morning*;
8 am–12 pm *Forenoon*; 12 pm–4 pm *Afternoon*;
4 pm–6 pm *First Dog*; 6 pm–8 pm *Second Dog*

*The charter instigating the United Nations was signed by its first intake of fifty-one member nations in San Francisco on 26 June 1945. The organisation officially came into existence when this manifesto was ratified on 24 October of that year. The charter then consisted of 111 articles with the following declaration of principles:*

WE THE PEOPLES
OF THE UNITED NATIONS
DETERMINED
to save succeeding generations from the scourge of war,
which twice in our lifetime has brought untold sorrow to mankind,
and to reaffirm faith in fundamental human rights, in the dignity
and worth of the human person, in the equal rights of men and
women and of nations large and small, and to establish conditions
under which justice and respect for the obligations arising
from treaties and other sources of international law can be
maintained, and to promote social progress and better standards
of life in larger freedom,
AND FOR THESE ENDS
to practice tolerance and live together in peace with one another as
good neighbours, and to unite our strength to maintain international
peace and security, and to ensure, by the acceptance of principles
and the institution of methods, that armed force shall not be used,
save in the common interest, and to employ international
machinery for the promotion of the economic and social
advancement of all peoples,
HAVE RESOLVED TO
COMBINE OUR EFFORTS TO
ACCOMPLISH THESE AIMS.

Accordingly, our respective Governments, through representatives
assembled in the city of San Francisco, who have exhibited their full
powers found to be in good and due form, have agreed to the present
Charter of the United Nations and do hereby establish an international organisation to be known as the United Nations.

Star of: *Francis*, 1949; *Francis Goes to the Races*, 1951; *Francis Goes to West Point*, 1952; *Francis Covers the Big Town*, 1953; *Francis Joins the Wacs*, 1954; *Francis in the Navy*, 1955\*; *Francis and the Haunted House*, 1956. The first six films were directed by Arthur Lubin, later the creator of television's 'Mr Ed', and the last by Charles Lamont.
\* Notable for second film appearance of Clint Eastwood.

## FOUNDATION DATES OF AUSTRALIAN NEWSPAPERS

*Adelaide Advertiser* 1858[1], *Age* 1854, *Australian* 1964, *Australian Financial Review* 1951, *Brisbane Courier-Mail*[2] 1846, *Geelong Advertiser* 1840, *Hobart Mercury* 1854, *Herald Sun* 1855[3], *Illawarra Mercury* 1855, *Sydney Morning Herald* 1831[4], *Telegraph–Mirror* 1879[5], *West Australian* 1833

---

1 Originally *South Australian Advertiser*; 2 Originally *Moreton Bay Courier*; 3 Originally *Herald*, merged with *Sun News-Pictorial*, 1990; 4 Originally *Sydney Herald*; 5 Originally *Daily Telegraph*, merged with *Mirror* 1990.

## ESSENTIAL MINERALS AND AMINO ACIDS

*Minerals:* calcium, magnesium, phosphorus, sodium, potassium, chlorine, iron, zinc, copper, manganese, molybdenum, fluorine, iodine, cobalt, chromium, selenium.
*Amino acids:* histidine, tryptophan, threonine, valine, phenylalanine, leucine, methionine, lysine, isoleusine.

## REPTILES OF THE ANTARCTIC

There are no reptiles in the Antarctic.

## ROYAL BYNAMES

Abbas the Great[1]—Alfred the Great[2]—Catherine the Great[3]—Charles the Affable[4]—Charles the Bald[4]—Charles the Fat[4]—Charles the Foolish[4]—Charles the Simple[4]—Edward the Confessor[2]—Edward the Martyr[2]—Ethelred the Unready[2]—Gorm the Old[5]—Hereward the Wake[2]—Ivan the Great[3]—Ivan the Terrible[3]—John the Blind[6]—Knut the Holy[5]—Louis the Pious[4]—Louis the Stammerer[4]—Magnus the Blind[7]—Olaf the Peaceful[7]—Pedro the Cruel[8]—Peter the Great[3]—Philip the Bold[9]—Philip the Fair[4]—Selim the Grim[10]—Thorfin the Skullsplitter[11]—Valdemar the Great[5]—Vlad the Impaler[12]—William the Conqueror[2]—Zygirant the Old[7]

1 Persia; 2 England; 3 Russia; 4 France; 5 Denmark; 6 Bohemia; 7 Norway; 8 Castile; 9 Spain; 10 Turkey/Ottoman Empire; 11 Viking; 12 Transylvania.

## THE NINE WORTHIES

Medieval list of the world's foremost warriors, designed, with ecumenical symmetry, to honour the three groups felt to have contributed most to the rise of the West. In his preface to Sir Thomas Malory's *Morte D'Arthur* (1485), for example, William Caxton wrote: 'For it is notoirly known through the universal world that there have been nine worthy and the best that ever were, that is to wit, three Paynims [pagans], three Jews and three Christian men.'

The Nine were: Hector of Troy, Alexander the Great, Julius Caesar, Joshua, King David, Judas Maccabaeus (Jewish warrior prince who routed the Hellenistic Syrians), King Arthur, Charlemagne and Godfrey of Bouillon (leader of the First Crusade).

*The crash of Korean Airlines Flight 007 near Sakhalin Island on 1 September 1983 remains shrouded in mystery. Mistaken for an American spy plane when it veered into Soviet airspace, the 747 was intercepted by a MiG pilot. This transcript of the cockpit voice recorder begins just as the aircraft was struck by a heat-seeking missile, and covers seven minutes in which it plunged 35,000 feet (10,668m) into the ocean.*

CAPTAIN: What happened?

CO-PILOT: What?

CAPTAIN: Retard throttles.

CO-PILOT: Engines normal.

CAPTAIN: Landing gear.

COCKPIT: [*Sound of cabin altitude warning.*]

CAPTAIN: Landing gear.

COCKPIT: [*Sound of altitude deviation warning; sound of autopilot disconnect warning.*]

CAPTAIN: Altitude is going up. Altitude is going up. Speed brake is coming out.

CO-PILOT: What? What?

CAPTAIN: Check it out.

COCKPIT: [*Sound of public address chime for automatic cabin announcement.*]

CO-PILOT: I am not able to drop altitude; now unable.

PUBLIC ADDRESS RECORDING: Attention, emergency descent.

CAPTAIN: Altitude is going up. This is not working. Manually.

CO-PILOT: Cannot do manually.

COCKPIT: Attention emergency descent [in Japanese]. [*Sound of autopilot disconnect warning.*]

CO-PILOT: Not working manually also. Engines are normal, sir.

PUBLIC ADDRESS RECORDING: Put out your cigarette. This is an emergency descent. Put out your cigarette. This is an emergency descent.

CAPTAIN: Is it power compression?

FLIGHT ENGINEER: Is that right?

PUBLIC ADDRESS RECORDING: Put out your cigarette. This is an emergency descent.

FLIGHT ENGINEER: All of both...

CAPTAIN: Is that right?

PUBLIC ADDRESS RECORDING: Put the mask over your nose and mouth, and adjust the headband.

CO-PILOT: Tokyo radio, Korean Air zero zero seven.

PUBLIC ADDRESS RECORDING: Put the mask over your nose and mouth, and adjust the headband.

TOKYO AIR TRAFFIC CONTROL: Korean Air zero zero seven, Tokyo.

PUBLIC ADDRESS RECORDING: Put the mask over your nose and mouth, and adjust the headband.

FLIGHT ENGINEER: All decompression.

CAPTAIN: Rapid decompression. Descend to one zero thousand [10,000 feet].

PUBLIC ADDRESS RECORDING: Attention, emergency descent. Attention, emergency descent.

FLIGHT ENGINEER: Now...we have to set this.

TOKYO AIR TRAFFIC CONTROL: Korean Air zero zero seven, radio check on one zero zero four eight.

PUBLIC ADDRESS RECORDING: Attention, emergency descent.

FLIGHT ENGINEER: Speed. Stand by. Stand by. Stand by. Stand by. Set.

PUBLIC ADDRESS RECORDING: Put out your cigarette. This is an emergency descent. Put out your cigarette. This is an emergency descent. Put out your cigarette. This is an emergency descent. Put the mask over your nose and mouth, and adjust the headband. Put the mask over your nose and mouth, and adjust... [Recording ends]

POLITICAL STRUCTURE OF OCEANIA

————•◆•————

*Big Brother* . . . . . . . . . . . . . . . . . . . . . . . . . . . . . omnipotent leader
*Thought Police* . . . . . . . . . . . . . . . . . . . omniscient supervisory force
*Inner Party* . . . . . . . . . . . . . . . . 'the brain of the state' formed of six
million members of the population of Oceania
*Outer Party* . . . . . . . . . . . . . . . . . . . . . . . . . . other ordinary citizens
*The Low/Proles* . . . . . . . . . . . . slave population, equatorial regions
*from George Orwell's* 1984 *(1948)*

In 1805 Royal Navy Commander (later Admiral) Francis Beaufort (1774–1857) devised his eponymous scale to describe the effect of wind on a man-of-war. The British Navy declared it mandatory in 1838 and it was expanded to include land conditions by the International Meteorological Committee in 1874. This confined the scale to effect rather than speed; the speeds of each number were not agreed upon until 1926. Beaufort's name is also attached to a sea at the edge of the Canadian Arctic Archipelago.

| Number | Symbol | Wind (knots) | Condition |
| --- | --- | --- | --- |
| 0 | ◎ | less than 1 | calm |
| 1 | | 1–3 | light air |
| 2 | | 4–6 | light breeze |
| 3 | | 7–10 | gentle breeze |
| 4 | | 11–16 | moderate breeze |
| 5 | | 17–21 | fresh breeze |
| 6 | | 22–27 | strong breeze |
| 7 | | 28–33 | near–moderate gale |
| 8 | | 34–40 | moderate gale |
| 9 | | 41–47 | strong gale |
| 10 | | 48–55 | storm |
| 11 | | 56–63 | violent storm |
| 12 | | 64+ | hurricane |

BEACHCOMBING

In the early 1990s, scientist Tim Benton visited an uninhabited atoll called Dulcie Island, the most remote of the Pitcairn Islands, 8000 kilometres east of Australia. He found on the beach the following 953 items of debris: unidentifiable pieces of plastic, 268; glass bottles, 171; bottle tops, 74; plastic bottles, 71; small buoys, 67; buoy fragments, 66; large buoys, 46; pieces of rope, 44; segments of plastic pipe, 29; shoes,

25; jars, 18; crates, 14; copper sheeting, 8; aerosol cans, 7; food and drink cans, 7; fluorescent tubes, 6; light bulbs, 6; jerry cans, 4; cigarette lighters, 3; pen tops, 2; dolls' heads, 2; gloves, 2 (a pair); asthma inhaler, 1; construction worker's hat, 1; football (punctured), 1; glue syringe, 1; truck tyre, 1; plastic coathanger, 1; plastic footmat, 1; plastic skittle, 1; small gas cylinder, 1; tea strainer, 1; tinned meat pie, 1; toy soldier, 1; toy aeroplane, 0.5.

## LA MARSEILLAISE

Often described as the most stirring of anthems, the Marseillaise was written as a marching song by an army engineer Claude-Joseph Rouget de Lisle in April 1792 to inspire troops for the coming war against Austria and Prussia, and entitled 'Chant de guerre pour l'armée du Rhin' ('War Song for the Rhine Army*). It was then published as 'Chant de guerre aux armées des frontières' ('Border Armies' War Song') by a revolutionary Francois Mireur seeking volunteers to march on Louis XVI's Tuileries Palace, and was sung so wholeheartedly by *sans-culottes* reaching the capital on 30 July 1792 that it became identified with them—ironically, as de Lisle himself was a monarchist. It became France's national song on 14 July 1795, and its national anthem eighty-four years later.

1

Arise children of the fatherland
The day of glory has arrived!
Against us tyranny's
Bloody standard is raised!
Listen to the sound in the fields,
The howling of these fearsome
  soldiers.
They are coming into our midst
To cut the throats of your sons
  and consorts.

*To arms citizens*
*Form your battalions*
*March, march*
*Let impure blood*
*Water our furrows*

## 2

What do they want this horde of
　　slaves,
Of traitors and conspiratorial
　　kings?
For whom these vile chains
These long-prepared irons?
Frenchmen, for us, ah! What
　　outrage,
What methods must be taken?
It is us they dare plan
To return to the old slavery!

## 3

What! These foreign cohorts!
They would make laws in our
　　courts!
What! These mercenary
　　phalanxes
Would cut down our warrior sons.
Good Lord! By chained hands
Our brow would yield under the
　　yoke.
The vile despots would have
　　themselves be
The masters of destiny.

## 4

Tremble, tyrants and traitors
The shame of all good men!
Tremble! Your parricidal
　　schemes
Will receive their just reward.
Against you we are all soldiers.
If they fall, our young heroes
France will bear new ones
Ready to join the fight against
　　you.

## 5

Frenchmen, as magnanimous
　　warriors
Bear or hold back your blows!
Spare these sad victims
That they regret taking up arms
　　against us!
But not these bloody despots
These accomplices of Bouillé
All these tigers who pitilessly
Ripped out their mothers' wombs.

## 6

We shall enter into the pit
When our elders will no longer
　　be there.
There we shall find their ashes
And the mark of their virtues.
We are much less jealous of
　　surviving them
Than of sharing their coffins.
We shall have the sublime pride
Of avenging or joining them.

## 7

Drive on sacred patriotism
Support our avenging arms!
Liberty! Cherished liberty,
Join the struggle with your
　　defenders!
Under our flags let victory
Hurry to your manly tone
So that in death your enemies
See your triumph and our glory!

*First Republic (1782–1804)*. . . . Outcome of the French Revolution.
*Second Republic (1848–52)* . . . . The interregnum between the fall of
Louis-Philippe and the Second Empire.
*Third Republic (1870–1940)*. . . . . The fall of Napoleon III until the
French surrender during World War II.
*Fourth Republic (1946–58)*. . . . Unstable period featuring twenty-six
governments finally undermined by instability in Algeria.
*Fifth Republic (1958–)*. . . . . . De Gaulle's presidency to the present.

## MORSE CODE

| | | | | | |
|---|---|---|---|---|---|
| A | • — | B | — • • • | C | — • — • |
| D | — • • | E | • | F | • • — • |
| G | — — • | H | • • • • | I | • • |
| J | • — — — | K | — • — | L | • — • • |
| M | — — | N | — • | O | — — — |
| P | • — — • | Q | — — • — | R | • — • |
| S | • • • | T | — | U | • • — |
| V | • • • — | W | • — — | X | — • • — |
| Y | — • — — | Z | — — • • | | |

| | | | | | |
|---|---|---|---|---|---|
| 1 | • — — — — | 2 | • • — — — | 3 | • • • — — |
| 4 | • • • • — | 5 | • • • • • | 6 | — • • • • |
| 7 | — — • • • | 8 | — — — • • | 9 | — — — — • |
| 10 | — — — — — | | | | |

## NOBLE EIGHTFOLD PATH OF BUDDHISM

Right views—Right intentions—Right speech—Right conduct—
Right livelihood—Right effort—Right mindfulness—Right concentration

## CATHOLIC CHURCH ORDER OF PRECEDENCE

Pope—Cardinal—Archbishop—Bishop—Monsignor—
Priest—Deacon

## SOME AMERICAN POLITICIANS WHO BECAME THE BASES FOR FICTIONAL CHARACTERS

Rutherford B. Hayes (1822–1893, 19th President)
'Old Granite' in *Democracy* by Henry Adams (1880).

Warren G. Harding (1863-1923, 29th President)
Willis Markham in *Revelry* by Samuel Adams (1926); Judson
Cumming Hammond in *Gabriel over the White House* by Thomas
Frederic Tweed (1933).

Zachary Taylor (1784–1850, 12th President)
'Old Blood and Thunder' in Nathaniel Hawthorne's short story
'The Great Stone Face' (1850).

Joseph R. McCarthy (1909–1957, Senator for Wisconsin)
John Iselin in *The Manchurian Candidate* by Richard Condon (1959).

Franklin D. Roosevelt (1882–1945, 32nd President)
Paul Hawley Barraclough in *The Politician* by Stephen and Ethel
Longstreet (1959).

Huey P. Long (1893–1935, Governor of and Senator for Louisiana)
Homer T. 'Chuck' Crawford in *Number One* by John dos Passos
(1943); Willie Stark in *All the King's Men* by Robert Penn Warren
(1946).

Dwight D. Eisenhower (1890–1969, 34th President)
Lucas P. Starbuck in *Hail to the Chief* by James Reichley (1960).

William J. B. Clinton Jnr (b. 1946, 42nd President)
Jack Stanton in *Primary Colours* by Anonymous (senior *Newsweek*
writer Joe Klein) (1996).

*Governor Stark's handshake in* All the King's Men:

He transferred his old gray hat to his left hand and took the two steps necessary to bring him to the table, and gravely extended his hand to me…I must have looked at his outstretched hand enquiringly and then given him a blank look, and he just showed me his dead pan…and kept on holding his hand out…It was a pretty good-sized hand. When you first took it you figured it was on the soft side, and the palm a little too moist—which is something, however, you don't hold against a man in certain latitudes—then you discovered it had a solid substructure. It was like the hand of a farm boy who has not too recently given up the plow for a job at the crossroads store. Willie's hand gave mine three decorous pump-handle motions, and he said, 'Glad to meetcha, Mr Burden,' like something he had memorized, and then, I could have sworn, he gave me a wink. Then, looking into that dead pan, I wasn't sure.

*Governor Stanton's handshake in* Primary Colours:

The handshake is the threshold act, the beginning of politics. I've seen him do it two million times now, but I couldn't tell you how he does it, the right-handed part of it—the strength, quality, duration of it, the rudiments of pressing the flesh. I can, however, tell you a whole lot about what he does with his other hand. He is a genius with it. He might put it on your elbow, or up to your biceps: these are basic, reflexive moves. He is interested in you. He is honoured to meet you. If he gets any higher up your shoulder—if he, say, drapes his left arm over your back, it is somehow less intimate, more casual. He'll share a laugh, or a secret, then—a light secret, not a real one—flattering you with the illusion of conspiracy. If he doesn't know you all that well and you've just told him something 'important', something earnest or emotional, he will lock in and honour you with a two-hander, his left hand overwhelming your wrist and forearm. He'll flash that famous misty look of his. And he will mean it.

———•·•———

*A coney.* . . . . . . . . . . . . . . . . . . . . . . . . . . . . . . . . . . . . . . . . . . . . . . a rabbit
*A fag* . . . . . . . . . . . . . . . . . . . . . . . a small stag following an old one
*To serve* . . . . . . . . . . . . . . . . . . . . . . . to mate a mare with a stallion
*A good lepper* . . . . . . . . . . . . . . . . . . . . . . . . . . . a good jumping horse
*A charley.* . . . . . . . . . . . . . . . . . . . . . . . . . . . . . . . . . . . . . . . . . . . . . . a fox
*Ware wire!* . . . . . . . . cry of warning to other riders when wire is seen
*Cock over.* . . . cry of beaters when cock pheasant is flushed from hiding
*To paunch* . . . . . . . . . . . . . . . . . . . . . . . . . . . . . . . . . . . to gut a rabbit
*Whipper-in* . . . . . . . . . . . . . . . . . Huntsman's assistant who prevents
hounds from straying
*A wormburner.* . . . . . . . . . . . . . . . . a pigeon released from traps flying
low at great speed
*Coffee housing* . . talking at the covert side and disturbing the hounds
*Currant jelly.* . . . . . . . . . . . the scent of a hare crossing the scent of a
fox and disturbing the hounds

## WIVES OF HENRY VIII

———•·•———

Catherine of Aragon—Anne Boleyn—Jane Seymour—Anne of
Cleves—Catherine Howard—Catherine Parr

*Divorced—Beheaded—Died—Divorced—Beheaded—Survived*

## HINTS TO GOLFERS

———•·•———

*The Great White Whale, 'one of the true legends of the game', confides
some secrets of the game to satirist John Clarke.*

- If your ball is in trouble, shift it.
- If there is water to the left of the fairway and safety to the right,
  don't take silly risks. Pull your front foot back about forty-five
  centimetres and hit your ball into the water.
- When you fail to get your weight through the ball properly, get your
  confidence back by banging the club repeatedly on the ground.

*Alliteration:* frequent occurrence in composition of words beginning with the same letter. *Acrostic:* a verse construction in which the first letters follow some predetermined order, usually a word, phrase or the alphabet. H. Southgate's *Many Thoughts on Many Things* contain these twenty-six lines, in which each word of each line begins with the letter of the alphabet it represents. They have been ascribed variously to Alaric Watts (1820) and Rev. B. Poulter (1828).

An Austrian army, awfully arrayed,
Boldly by battery besieged Belgrade;
Cossack commanders cannonading come,
Dealing destruction's devastating doom;
Every endeavour engineers essay
For fame, for fortune, forming furious fray.
Gaunt gunner grapple, giving gashes good;
Heaves high his head, heroic hardihood;
Ibraham, Islam, Ismael, imps in ill,
Jostle John Jarovlitz, Jem, Joe, Jack, Jill;
Kick kindling Kutusoff, kings' kinsmen kill
Labour low levels loftiest, longest lines;
Men march 'mid moles, 'mid mounds, 'mid murd'rous mines.
Now nightfall's near, now needful nature nods,
Opposed, opposing, overcoming odds.
Poor peasants, partly purchased, partly pressed.
Quite quaking, 'Quarter! Quarter!' quickly quest.
Reason returns, recalls redundant rage,
Saves sinking soldiers, softens signiors sage.
Truce, Turkey, truce! Truce, treach'rous Tartar train!
Unwise, unjust, unmerciful Ukraine,
Vanish, vile vengeance! Vanish, victory vain!
Wisdom wails war—wails warring words. What were
Xerxes, Xantippê, Ximenês, Xavier?
Yet Yassy's youth, ye yield your youthful yest.
Zealously, zanies, zealously, zeal's zest.

Of his predecessor, Sir William McMahon: 'Tiberius with a telephone.'

Of Malcolm Fraser's appointment as 'caretaker' prime minister: 'It must be the first time a burglar has been appointed caretaker.'

Of a Liberal navy minister: 'The man is of lesser calibre but a bigger bore.'

Of Sam Cohen, Labor's deputy leader in the Senate: 'Sam is always caught in a conflict of disloyalties.'

On the Soviet Union's support for tours by the Bolshoi Ballet: 'We do not send our artists overseas. We drive them away for good.'

Of himself: 'It's not for me to claim that I was a good prime minister, but as a realist I now must accept the universal claim that I was the best.'

Said when, during an austerity drive, his government colleagues jibed at travelling economy class: 'Most of the people round this table are pissants, and they can travel first class for the rest of their lives and they'll still be pissants. I, on the other hand, could travel economy class forever and still be a great man.'

On revealing three books kept together on his bookshelf: 'The Bible, *The Complete Works of William Shakespeare* and *The Whitlam Government*.'

## THE SEVEN WONDERS OF THE WORLD

### I. THE GREAT PYRAMID (GIZA, EGYPT)

The oldest and only surviving wonder is the largest of Egypt's eighty pyramids, built in honour of the Egyptian Pharoaoh Khufu about 2560 B.C. Located just outside of Cairo on the west bank of the Nile, and flanked by the slightly smaller pyramids of Khafra and Menkaura, it contains about 2.3 million blocks of quarried limestone, some weighing almost three tonnes. It is 230 metres long each side and, although erosion and damage have reduced its original height by ten metres to about 135 metres, remained the world's tallest structure until the nineteenth century. The effort involved in the pyramids' construction—Herodotus was told that as many as 100,000 men were involved—has beggared the belief of scholars since. Egyptologist Kurt Mendelssohn notes in *The Riddle of the Pyramids* (1974): 'The pyramids of Egypt are immensely large, immensely ancient and by general consensus, extremely useless.' He concludes: 'What mattered was not the pyramid but building the pyramid.'

## 2. THE HANGING GARDENS (BABYLON, IRAQ)

Details are scarce regarding what were said to be terrace gardens atop arches twenty-three metres above ground level sustained by the rerouted water of the Euphrates. They are ascribed to Nebuchadnezzar II, who is said to have commissioned them around 562 B.C. to ease the homesick pinings of a royal bride from lush and mountainous Medes. Archaeologists have found evidence of a man-made mountain and a system for providing artificial rain, although there remains dispute about where the site was located. The visiting Pliny the Elder found them in ruins about A.D. 70.

## 3. THE STATUE OF ZEUS (OLYMPIA, GREECE)

Constructed about 430 B.C. from ivory and gold by the Athenian Phedias—also one of the decorators of the temple at Ephesus—the statue of a seated Zeus stood thirteen metres tall and was enclosed in a multicoloured temple near the site of the ancient Olympics (then held every five years). His eyes were jewels, his throne footstool gold. The statue defied Caligula's demands that it be brought to Rome in the first century, but not a plan to move it east after the temple was closed when the Olympics were outlawed as a pagan practice in A.D. 391. It reposed in a palace in Constantinople for seventy years before being destroyed by fire.

## 4. THE TEMPLE OF DIANA (EPHESUS, TURKEY)

Philon of Byzantium, the mathematician who first surveyed the Seven Wonders, thought the temple in the Ionian city of Ephesus most spectacular: 'But when I saw the temple at Ephesus rising to the clouds, all these other wonders were put in the shade.' Commissioned by Croeus in about 550 B.C., the marble temple featured 127 20-metre-high columns and was decorated by a host of bronzes, including a statue of Diana, goddess of hunting. St Paul denounced it in the New Testament, stating that 'the temple of the Great Diana should be despised, and her magnificence should be destroyed'. After two centuries it was indeed seriously damaged by an arsonist, though it was the Goths who finally razed it to the ground in A.D. 262.

## 5. THE TOMB OF KING MAUSSOLLUS (HALICARNASSUS, TURKEY)

The inaugural mausoleum, in the Persian province of Caria, was commissioned by Queen Artemisia upon the death in 353 B.C. of her husband/brother Maussollus, after she had first drunk his ashes in a cup of wine. The rectangular sculpted marble tomb, surrounded by thirty-six Ionic columns supporting an architrave that bore a statue of the monarchs in a chariot, took three years to build. An earthquake damaged the roof and colonnade after 1900 years, and the Knights of St John of Malta fortified a crusader castle with stones from the tomb.

## 6. THE COLOSSUS (RHODES, THE AEGEAN SEA)

This thirty-three-metre-high nude of Apollo, constructed of stone and iron plated with bronze, was designed for Rhodians by Chares of Lindos to celebrate the lifting of a twelve-year siege by Ptolemy I of Macedonia and erected on its marble base in about 260 B.C. Cassius's famous allusion in Shakespeare's *Julius Caesar*—'He doth bestride this narrow world like a Colossus'—is misleading: the statue stood with feet together on a promontory at the harbour entrance. Badly damaged by an earthquake after less than forty years, it was never restored, on the advice of an oracle. Invading Arabs sold the 327,000 kg of stone, iron and bronze to a scrap merchant, who needed 900 camels to freight it to Syria.

## 7. THE PHAROS (OFF ALEXANDRIA, EGYPT)

A 117-metre lighthouse designed by Sostratus of Cnidus on the orders of Ptolemy Soter in 290 B.C., though not completed until the reign of his son Ptolemy Philadelphus. Erected on a small island and topped with an image of Poseidon, it relied for illumination on a huge brazier and reflecting mirror visible almost 500 kilometres from shore. Weakened by earthquakes in 956, 1303 and 1323, its stone was plundered for a medieval fort by Egypt's Sultan Qaitby in 1480.

*Solids*

Tetrahedron 4 faces (below); Hexahedron 6 faces; Octahedron 8 faces; Dodecahedron 12 faces; Icosahedron 20 faces.

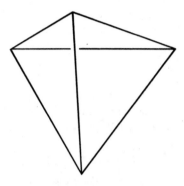

*Semi-Regular Solids*

Cuboctahedron/Dymaxion 12 corners, 14 faces; Truncated Octahedron/ Mecon 24 corners, 14 faces; Rhombicuboctahedron/Square Spin 24 corners, 26 faces; Snub Cube 24 corners, 38 faces; Icosidodecahedron 30 corners, 32 faces; Truncated Cuboctahedron 48 corners, 26 faces (below); Rhombicosidodecahedron 60 corners, 62 faces; Snub Dodecahedron 60 corners, 92 faces; Truncated Icosidodecahedron 120 corners, 62 faces.

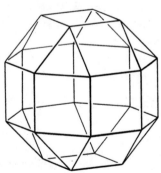

*Addison's Disease*
Thomas Addison, English physician (1795–1860)
Progressive destruction of adrenal gland caused by hormonal deficiency.

*Alzheimer's Disease*
Alois Alzheimer, German neuropathologist and psychiatrist (1864–1915)
Chronic, progressive, organic mental disease due to atrophy of the frontal and occipital lobes causing presenile dementia.

*Crohn's Disease*
Bernard Burrill Crohn, American gastroenterologist (1884–1983)
Subacute, chronic intestinal inflammation.

*Da Costa's Disease*
Jacob Mendez da Costa, American internist (1833–1900)
Effort fatigue, palpitation and other symptoms of nervousness, commonly seen in servicemen under stress.

*Huntington's Chorea*
George Sumner Huntington, American physician (1850–1916)
Disease of the nervous system characterised by progressive dementia with grimacing, gesticulation, speech disorders and other involuntary movements.

*Morton's Neuralgia*
Thomas Morton, American surgeon (1835–1903)
Sudden cramps in the metatarsal area, usually the fourth and fifth toes.

*Osgood-Schlatter's Disease*
Robert Bayley Osgood, American orthopaedic surgeon (1873–1956); Carl B. Schlatter (1864–1934), Swiss physician
Osteochondrosis of the tuberosity of the tibia causing knee pain, most common in adolescents.

*Parkinson's Disease*
James Parkinson, English physician (1755–1824)
Degenerative neurological affliction marked by worsening tremor.

*Reiter's Disease*
Hans Conrad Julius Reiter, German bacteriologist and hygienist
(1881–1969)
Combination urethritis, arthritis and conjunctivitis, in sexually transmitted and post-dysenteric forms.

*Takayasu's Disease*
Mikito Takayasu, Japanese ophthalmologist (1860–1938)
Inflammation of the aorta which occludes one or more branches of the
aortic arch.

BENFORD'S LAW

This phenomenological law, also known as 'the leading digit phenomenon', states that in a wide variety of circumstances—ranging from
populations to properties of chemicals, newspaper circulations to street
addresses—the digit 1 occurs with disproportionate probability. In truly
random statistical series '1' would occur 11.1 per cent of the time (that
is, one digit out of 9). It is generally closer to 30 per cent; '2' appears
about 18 per cent of time; '3' about 12.5 per cent; '9' less than 5 per cent.

Astronomer Simon Newcomb, in his 'Note on the Frequency of the
Use of Digits in Natural Numbers' in the *American Journal of
Mathematics* in 1881, observed that books of logarithm tables were far
dirtier and more scuffed at the front, indicating that people looked
more frequently at lower numbers. This concept was rediscovered and
advanced as a law fifty-seven years later by physicist Frank Benford in
'The Law of Anomalous Numbers', in the *Proceedings of the American
Philosophical Society*, although only recently was it established which
sort of situations generate numbers in accordance with the law and
which do not. Benford's Law applies to data that are *not* dimension-
less, so the numerical values of the data depend on the units. Both the
laws of physics and human convention impose cut-offs: tax returns
and financial data, for instance, all seem to observe Benford's Law. In
1995 Georgia Tech mathematician Ted Hill explored the law most
thoroughly in his paper 'The Significant-Digit Phenomenon' in
*American Mathematics Monthly*.

For I will consider my Cat Jeoffry/For he is the servant of the Living
God duly and daily serving him.../For he will not do destruction, if he
is well-fed, neither will he spit without provocation/For he purrs in
thankfulness, when God tells him he's a good Cat/For he is an instru-
ment for the children to learn benevolence upon/For every house is
incompleat without him and a blessing is lacking in the spirit.

from 'Jubilate Agno' by Christopher Smart (1722–1771)[1]

*Appolinaris, Beelzebub, Blatherskaite, Buffalo Bill**...... Mark Twain
(1835–1910), American author/humorist

*Beppo* ......... Jose Luis Borges (1899–1986), Argentinian author

*Bismarck*........ Florence Nightingale (1820–1910), English nurse

*Blackie, Jock, Nelson, Tango** ...... Winston Churchill (1874–1965),
British prime minister

*Chess, Checkmate* ... Aleksander Alekhine (1892–1946), chess master

*Cobby* ................. Thomas Hardy (1840–1928), novelist

*Fuckchop* ...... Trent Reznor (1965– ), lead singer Nine Inch Nails

*George Pushdragon**........... T. S. Eliot (1888–1965), poet, critic

*Gujarat*[2] ........... John Kenneth Galbraith (1908– ), economist

*Langbourne* .... Jeremy Bentham (1748–1832), British philosopher

*Mrs Chippy* ......... ship's cat on the *Endurance* expedition, 1914

*Nigeraurak* ........... ship's cat on the *Karluk* expedition, 1913

*Siam*[3] ...... Rutherford B. Hayes (1822–1893), 19th US President

*Taki*..... Raymond Chandler (1888–1959), American crime writer

*Trim* .. ship's cat on the *Investigator*'s circumnavigation of Australia,
1801–1803

---

* and others.

1 Poem written 'between 1758 and 1763, largely while in a mad-
house'; Smart's mania took the form of compulsive praying, and
trying to get his friends to do the same.

2 Name changed from 'Ahmedabad' when Indian officials complained
during Galbraith's period as ambassador.

3 The first Siamese cat to reach the US in 1878, a gift from his
consul in Bangkok.

*Star (distance in light years)*
Proxima Centauri (4.28); Alpha Centauri A, B (4.3); Barnard's Star (5.9); Wolf 359 (7.8); Lalande 21185 (8.2); Sirius A, B (8.7); UV Ceti A, B (8.8); Ross 154 (9.4); Ross 248 (10.4); Epsilon Eradini (10.8); Ross 128 (10.8); Cygnus A, B (11.1).

## PHOBIAS

being housebound *domatophobia*

blushing *erythrophobia*

body odour *bromidrosiphobia*

bridges *gephyrophobia*

busy streets *agyiophobia*

cats *ailurophobia*

childbirth *maieusiophobia*[1]

clowns *coulrophobia*

dogs *cynophobia*

dirt *miasmophobia*

falling downstairs *climacophobia*

falling satellites *keraunothen-tophobia*

frogs *ranidaphobia*

gaiety *cherophobia*

justice *dikephobia*

kissing *philematophobia*

lightning *keraunophobia*

marriage *gamophobia*

mirrors *kathreptophobia*[2]

missiles *ballistophobia*

parents-in-law *soceraphobia*

pins *belonephobia*

popes *papaphobia*

remaining single *anuptaphobia*

responsibility *hypengyophobia*[3]

ridicule *catagelophobia*

riding in cars *amaxophobia*

sharks *karkharaphobia*

sitting *cathisophobia*

stepfathers *vitricophobia*

thirteen *treiskaidekaphobia*

thunderstorms *brontophobia*

tickling *pteronophobia*[4]

tombstones *placophobia*

tornadoes *lilapsophobia*

virgins *parthenophobia*

worm infestation *helminthophobia*

1 also known as *tocophobia;* 2 also known as *spectrophobia*; 3 also known as *paraliphobia;* 4 esp with feathers.

## TWENTY-FIVE POLITICAL ASSASSINATIONS

| Victim | Perpetrator | Date | Place | Circumstances |
|---|---|---|---|---|
| Philip II (King of Macedon, father of Alexander the Great) | Pausanias | August 336 B.C. | Pella | Stabbed by a bodyguard at a state ceremony. |
| Gaius Julius Caesar (Roman *imperator perpetuum*) | Marcus Junius Brutus/ Gaius Cassius Longinus and others | 15 March 44 B.C. | Rome | Stabbed while taking his seat in the Senate.[1] |
| William the Silent (Dutch *pater patriae*) | Balthazar Gerards | 15 July 1584 | Delft | Shot on a stairwell as he emerged from his dining room. |
| Gustav III (King of Sweden) | Jacob Johan Anckarström | 16 March 1792 | Stockholm | Shot in the back during masquerade ball at Royal Castle; died 29 March.[2] |
| Jean-Paul Marat (editor of Jacobin journal *L'Ami du peuple*) | Charlotte Corday | 13 July 1793 | Paris | Stabbed while having his daily bath, which he took to soothe a skin condition.[3] |

48

| | | | | |
|---|---|---|---|---|
| Spencer Perceval (British prime minister) | John Bellingham | 11 May 1812 | London | Shot once in the chest while crossing the lobby of the House of Commons. |
| Abraham Lincoln (American president) | John Wilkes Booth | 14 April 1865 | Washington | Shot from behind in the presidential box at Ford's Theatre. [4 & 5] |
| Alexander II (Russian czar) | Members of anarchist group The People's Will | 13 March 1881 | St Petersburg | Blown up while returning to the Winter Palace from a military parade. |
| James Garfield (American president) | Charles Guiteau[4] | 2 July 1881 | Washington | Shot in a railway waiting room at close range; died in Elberon 19 September 1881. |
| Humbert I (King of Italy) | Angelo Bresci | 30 July 1900 | Monza | Shot in the chest three times at close range. |
| William McKinley (American president) | Leon Czolgosz[4] | 6 September 1901 | Buffalo | Shot at close range while opening an exhibition. |

| Victim | Perpetrator | Date | Place | Circumstances |
|---|---|---|---|---|
| George I (King of Greece) | Alexander Schinas | 18 March 1913 | Salonika | Shot while taking his daily constitutional. |
| Franz Ferdinand & Duchess of Hohenburg (Austro-Hungarian archduke and wife) | Gavrilo Princip | 28 June 1914 | Sarajevo | Shot at close range while driving in a motorcade. |
| Alexander (King of Yugoslavia) | Petrus Keleman | 9 October 1934 | Marseilles | Shot at close range from the running board of a car. |
| Leon Trotsky (Russian ideologue in exile) | Ramon Mercader | 21 August 1940 | Mexico City | Skull crushed by an ice pick. |
| Mohandas Gandhi (Indian independence campaigner) | Nathuram Godse | 30 January 1948 | New Delhi | Shot three times at close range while moving through a crowd.[6] |
| Patrice Lumumba (first prime minister of the Congo) | Unknown Congolese secessionists | 17 January 1961 | Elizabethville | Probably shot; body never found.[7] |

| Name | Assassin | Date | Place | Details |
|---|---|---|---|---|
| John Kennedy (American president) | Lee Harvey Oswald | 22 November 1963 | Dallas | Shot while riding in a motorcade in Dealy Plaza.[4 & 8] |
| Hendrik Verwoerd (South African prime minister) | Demetrio Tsafendas | 6 September 1966 | Pretoria | Stabbed four times in the chest with a long stiletto. |
| Martin Luther King (American civil rights leader) | James Earl Ray | 4 April 1968 | Memphis | Ray escaped after firing lethal shots and was arrested in London on 8 June.[9] |
| Robert Kennedy (American senator) | Sirhan Sirhan | 5 June 1968 | Los Angeles | Shot with a hand gun five times at close range. |
| Anwar el-Sadat (Egyptian president) | Members of Islamic Jihad | 6 October 1981 | Cairo | Shot by automatic fire from five assassins. |
| Indira Gandhi (Indian prime minister) | Beant Singh/ Sukwhant Singh | 31 October 1984 | New Delhi | Shot by Sikh bodyguards. |

| Victim | Perpetrator | Date | Place | Circumstances |
| --- | --- | --- | --- | --- |
| Olof Palme (Swedish prime minister) | Unknown (suspect Christer Petterson acquitted on appeal) | 28 February 1986 | Stockholm | Shot while walking home from a cinema with his wife. |
| Nicolae Ceausescu (Romanian dictator) | Firing squad of Romanian Salvation Front | 25 December 1989 | Bucharest | Shot after a brief trial by military court. |
| Yitzhak Rabin (Israeli prime minister) | Yigal Amir | 4 November 1995 | Tel Aviv | Shot twice while returning to his car after a peace rally. |

1 Subject of play, *Julius Caesar* (1599), by William Shakepeare; 2 Subject of opera, *Un Ballo in Maschera* (1859), by Giuseppe Verdi; 3 Subject of painting, *Death of Marat* (1794), by Jacques-Louis David; 4 Featured in musical, *Assassins* (1990), by Stephen Sondheim and John Weidman; 5 Subject of poem, 'O Captain! My Captain!' (1871), by Walt Whitman; Lincoln was watching the comedy *Our American Cousin* (1858) by Tom Taylor; 6 Subject of films *Nine Hours to Rama* (1963) directed by Mark Robson, *Hey Ram* (2000) directed by Kamal Hasan, and play *Me Nathuram Godse Boltoy* (1989) by Pradeep Dalavi; 7 Subject of movie *Lumumba* (2001) directed by Raoul Peck; 8 Subject of movie *JFK* (1991) directed by Oliver Stone, song '22 November 1963' (1981) by New Race, and novels *Libra* (1989) by Don De Lillo, *Flying in to Love* (1992) by D. M. Thomas, *Idlewild* (1993) by Mark Lawson, *American Tabloid* (1995) and *The Cold Six Thousand* (2002) by James Ellroy, *The Invisible World* (2002) by John Smolens. For Oswald, see the song 'The Shah Sleeps in Lee Harvey's Grave' (1984) by Butthole Surfers and the book *Oswald's Tale: An American Mystery* (1996) by Norman Mailer; 9 Subject of song, 'Pride (in the Name of Love)', by U2 (1984).

*According to American theologian Paul Tillich (1886–1965) in his 1952 book* The Courage to Be, *anxiety is of three distinct kinds:*

ONTIC ANXIETY: the anxiety of fate and death.

MORAL ANXIETY: the anxiety of guilt and condemnation.

SPIRITUAL ANXIETY: the anxiety of emptiness and meaninglessness.

## POPULAR KNOTS

*Slip knot*

*Bowline*

*Fisherman's knot*

*Reef knot*

*In June 1835, a group of Tasmanian merchant venturers called the Port Phillip Association led by grazier John Batman acquired the land on which Melbourne now resides from the Dutigallar tribe, which involved the signing of the following deed by Batman, his colleagues and the tribal chiefs.*

Know all persons that we, three brothers, Jagajaga, Jagajaga, Jagajaga, being the three principal chiefs, and also Cooloolock, Bungarie, Yanyan, Moowhip, Monmarmalar, being the chiefs of a certain native tribe called Dutigallar, situate at and near Port Phillip, called by us, the above-mentioned chiefs, Iramoo, being possessed of the tract of land hereinafter mentioned for and in consideration of twenty pairs of blankets, thirty tomahawks, one hundred knives, fifty pairs scissors, thirty looking-glasses, two hundred handkerchiefs, and one hundred pounds of flour, and six shirts, delivered to us by John Batman, residing in Van Diemen's Land, Esquire, but at present sojourning with us and our tribe, do for ourselves, our heirs and successors give grant enfeoff and confirm unto the said John Batman, his heirs and assigns, all that tract of country situate and being at Port Phillip, running from the branch of the river at the top of the port, about seven miles from the mouth of the river, forty miles north-east, and from thence, west, forty miles across Iramoo Downs or Plains and from thence south-south-west, across Mount Vilaumanartar to Geelong Harbour at the head of the same and containing 500,000 more or less acres, as the same hath been before the execution of these presents delineated and marked out by us according to the custom of our tribe by certain marks made upon the trees growing along the boundaries of the said tract of land, to hold the said tract of land, with all advantages belonging thereto, unto and to the use of the said John Batman, his heirs and assigns for ever, to the intent that the said John Batman his heirs and assigns may occupy and possess the said tract of land and place thereon sheep and cattle. Yielding and delivering to us, and our heirs or successors the yearly rent or tribute of one hundred pairs of blankets, one hundred knives, one hundred tomahawks, fifty suits of clothing, fifty looking-glasses, fifty pairs scissors and five tons of flour.

In witness thereof, we, Jagajaga, Jagajaga, Jagajaga, the before mentioned principal chiefs, and Cooloolock, Bungarie, Yanyan, Moowhip, and Monmarmalar, the chiefs of the said tribe, have hereunto affixed our seals to these presents, and have signed the same. Dated according to the Christian era, this sixth day of June, 1835.

Signed, sealed and delivered in the presence of us the same having been fully and properly interpreted and explained to the said chiefs.

John Batman
James Gumm
Alexander Thompson
Willm. Todd

Jagajaga
Jagajaga
Jagajaga
Cooloolock
Bungarie
Yanyan
Moowhip
Monmarmalar

## YIDDISH PUTDOWNS

———◆◆◆———

*Kibbitzer* a heckler—*Klutz* a bungler—*Narr* a fool—*Nebbish* a dope—*Nudnick* a bore—*Putz** a simpleton—*Shlemiel* a complete dope—*Shlimazl* a born loser—*Shlub* a rude bungler—*Shmegegge* a groveller—*Shmendrick* a wimp—*Shmo/Shmuck** a complete jerk—*Shnook* a sap.

\* Also means 'penis'.

## PARRHESIA

———◆◆◆———

Notably candid or blunt address which a speaker would not normally be positioned to make. Thus the prophet Nathan's admonition of King David in 2 Samuel 12: 'Then David's anger was greatly kindled against the man, and he said to Nathan, "As the Lord lives, the man who has done this deserves to die…" Nathan said to David, "You are the man."'

Conceived in 1851 at the Great Exhibition and finally launched in 1858, the *Great Eastern* was the largest ship of its time and some time after: its displacement, 6000 tonnes greater than the *Titanic*, was not exceeded for half a century (by the *Lusitania*). The first large vessel designed without ribs, the *Great Eastern*'s twin hulls were riveted together from iron plates and split into sixteen compartments by longitudinal and transverse bulkheads. She weighed more than the 197 ships in the English fleet that opposed the Spanish Armada put together, and was so huge that she had to be constructed on a Thames riverbank—there being no dry dock large enough to accommodate the project. Her measurements were as follows: *Length:* 692 feet (209.7 m); *Beam:* 120 feet (36.3 m); *Displacement:* 22,500 tonnes; *Maximum passenger complement:* 4000; *Masts:* 6, carrying 65,000 square yards of sail; *Funnels:* five from ten boilers drawing on 15,000 tonnes of coal, creating 11,000 horsepower to turn two 58-foot paddlewheels (17.5 m) and one 24-foot screw (7.2 m) (still the largest in history). The *Great Eastern*'s lifespan was dogged by misfortune. Her designer Isambard Brunel (1806–1859) had a stroke while on board just before her maiden voyage; her captain had a nervous breakdown after it. She suffered four mutinies, sank four other ships in collisions, was involved in thirteen legal actions and was auctioned six times. The pinnacle of her accomplishments was laying the transatlantic telegraph cable; the low point her conversion to a floating circus shortly before she went to the breakers in 1887.

## CHARACTERS IN LANGUAGE

Chinese 40–50,000 (ideographic characters); Japanese 18,000 (ideographic characters); Khmer/Cambodian 74 (alphabetic characters); Sanskrit 48; Cyrillic 33; Persian 32; Turkish 29; Spanish 29; Arabic 28; German 27; English 26; French 26; Greek 24; Hebrew 22; Early Latin 21, Hawaiian 12.

Mr Fantastic—The Thing—The Invisible Girl—The Human Torch

## FOREIGN WORDS FOR LEADER

*archon* (Greek) . . . . . . . . . . . . . . . . . . . . . . . . . . . . chief magistrate*
*bey* (Turkish) . . . . . . . . . . . . . . . . . . . . . . . . . . . . . . . . . . . . . chief
*burgermeister* (German) . . . . . . . . . . . . . . . . . . . . . . . . . . . . mayor
*bwana* (Swahili) . . . . . . . . . . . . . . . . . . . . . . . . . . . . . . . . . . . . boss
*caliph* (Arabic) . . . . . . . . . . . . . . . . . . . . . . . . . . . . . . . successor
*capo* (Italian) . . . . . . . . . . . . . . . . . . . . . . . . . . . . . . . . . . . . . head
*commissar* (Russian) . . . . . . . . . . . . . . . . . . . . . . . . . . party boss
*czar* (Russian) . . . . . . . . . . . . . . . . . . . . . . . . . . . . . . . . emperor
*duce* (Italian) . . . . . . . . . . . . . . . . . . . . . . . . . . . . . . . . . . . . duke
*emir* (Arabic) . . . . . . . . . . . . . . . . . . . . . . . . . . . . . . commander
*Fuhrer* (German) . . . . . . . . . . . . . . . . . . . . . . . . . . . . . . . leader
*generalisimo* (Spanish) . . . . . . . . . . . . . . . . . . commander-in-chief
*guru* (Sanskrit) . . . . . . . . . . . . . . . . . . . . . . . . . . . . . . . . teacher
*honcho* (Japanese) . . . . . . . . . . . . . . . . . . . . . . . . . . squad leader
*Kaiser* (German) . . . . . . . . . . . . . . . . . . . . . . . . . . . . . . emperor
*khan* (Turkish) . . . . . . . . . . . . . . . . . . . . . . . . . . . . . . . . . prince
*mikado* (Japanese) . . . . . . . . . . . . . . . . . . . . . . . . . . . . emperor
*nabob* (Hindi) . . . . . . . . . . . . . . . . . . . . . . . . . . . . . . . governor
*pontifex* (Latin) . . . . . . . . . . . . . . . . . . . . . . . . . . . . . . . . priest
*rajah* (Hindi) . . . . . . . . . . . . . . . . . . . . . . . . . . . . . . . . . . . king
*sahib* (Hindi) . . . . . . . . . . . . . . . . . . . . . . . . . . . . . . . . . . . boss
*satrap* (Greek) . . . . . . . . . . . . . . . . . . . . . . . . . . . . . . governor
*sensei* (Japanese) . . . . . . . . . . . . . . . . . . . . . . . . . . . . . teacher
*shogun* (Japanese) . . . . . . . . . . . . . . . . . . . . . . . . . . . . warlord
*vizier* (Turkish) . . . . . . . . . . . . . . . . . . . . . . . . . executive officer

* Thus 'anarchy' in his absence.

### YORICK

The first living creature launched and successfully recovered, Yorick, a monkey (breed unknown), lifted off from the Holloman Air Force Base in New Mexico aboard an Aerobee booster on 20 September 1951. Accompanied by eleven mice, Yorick attained an altitude of 72 kilometres.

### PATRICIA/MIKE

Two Philippine monkeys launched aboard an Aerobee from Holloman on 22 May 1952. They were watched on a video camera as they soared to a height of 57.6 kilometres and at speeds of up to 3200 km/h. Mike was strapped in a prone position, Patricia upright; two mice were set loose in a clear holding drum, where they became weightless. All the animals survived. Patricia and Mike retired to Washington's National Zoological Park.

### LAIKA (Barker)

A three-year-old Russian mongrel bitch, mostly Siberian husky, was launched with *Sputnik* 2 from the Baikonur Cosmodrome on 3 November 1957. She had been found as a stray on the streets of Moscow, and was also known to her handlers as Kudryavka (Little Curly); American pressmen dubbed her 'Muttnik'. Transmissions lasted seven days, until oxygen ran out, and her remains were incinerated when *Sputnik* 2 re-entered after 2370 orbits in 103 days. In the statue honouring lives lost in the Soviet space program at Star City in Moscow, Laika peers out from behind a group of cosmonauts.

### GORDO

A squirrel monkey launched aboard a Jupiter AM-13 booster by the US Army on 13 December 1958, part of a panicky American response to the success of the Sputniks. The flight was completed successfully, but Gordo drowned when the flotation device in the capsule's nose cone failed.

SAM

A rhesus monkey, named for School of Aviation Medicine at Brooks Air Force Base, San Antonio, travelled in a Mercury capsule on Little Joe test flight from Wallops Island on 4 December 1959. Experienced four minutes of weightlessness in suborbital flight reaching 88 kilometres. Returned to the laboratory, he reportedly hugged his unrelated rhesus monkey colleague Miss Sam, who herself undertook a brief 20-kilometre flight a month later to test the Mercury capsule's escape mechanism.

BELKA (Squirrel)/STRELKA (Little Arrow)

Launched with *Sputnik* 5 from Baikonur Cosmodrome on 19 August 1960. The second trial of the Vostok capsule which would carry Yuri Gagarin into space the following April; it also carried forty mice, two rats and several plants. The two dogs were ejected after eighteen orbits in a pressurised capsule which was successfully recovered. Strelka later gave birth to six puppies, one of which was given to US president John F. Kennedy.

HAM

A four-year-old American chimpanzee launched in Mercury capsule atop a Redstone booster, from Cape Canaveral on 31 January 1961. Named for the Holloman Aerospace Medical Center in New Mexico, and also for its commanding officer Lt. Col. Hamilton Blackshear. The flight required Ham to manipulate control levers in return for banana pellets, which he did, despite a stressful flight reaching speeds of almost 10,000 km/h, involving almost seven minutes of weightlessness and overshooting the recovery area by 200 kilometres. Ham retired from duties on 2 April 1963 to Washington's National Zoological Park.

CHERNUSHKA (Blackie)

Launched with *Sputnik* 9 from Baikonur Cosmodrome on 9 March 1961, Chernushka, a black dog, was successfully recovered the same day. The fourth trial of Vostok capsule also carried a dummy cosmonaut, a guinea pig and several mice.

ZVEZDOCHKA (Little Star)

Launched with *Sputnik* 10 from Baikonur Cosmodrome on 25 March 1961. Fifth and final trial of Vostok capsule. Zvezdochka, a white dog, was successfully recovered after one orbit. Cosmonaut Yuri Gagarin performed the same feat eighteen days later. With Laika, Belka, Strelka and Chernushka, Zvezdochka has been featured on a Bulgarian stamp.

ENOS

The first primate in orbit, an American chimpanzee launched in a Mercury capsule atop an Atlas 5 booster from Cape Canaveral on 29 November 1961. The flight was aborted after two of a planned three orbits due to system problems, though Enos discharged all his duties successfully. His fondness for masturbating, which scientists tried to prevent with a catheter, and with which he delighted his press conference, earned him the nickname 'Enos the Penis'. He died a year later of an unrelated infection. John Glenn became first American human in orbit on 20 February 1962.

FELIX

A stray black-and-white tomcat plucked from the streets of Paris by France's Centre d'Enseignment et de Recherches de Medecine Aeronautique (CERMA) and launched in the nose cone of a Veronique AGI sounding rocket from the Hammaguir Testing Range in Algeria on 18 October 1963. Felix was recovered successfully after reaching a height of almost 200 kilometres, but another cat launched six days later perished. (Some sources give Felix as Felicette.)

VERTEROK (Little Wind)/UGOLYOK (Little Piece of Coal)

Russian dogs launched aboard the biosatellite *Kosmos* 110 (also known as *Voskhod* 3) from Baikonur Cosmodrome on 22 February 1966. Their twenty-two-day flight, observed by video and biomedical telemetry, remains the non-human endurance record, and was not surpassed by humans until the first Skylab flight (twenty-eight days) in July 1974.

*Other creatures which have travelled in space: fish, frogs, newts, rats, snails, spiders and worms.*

————•◦•————

*Akron:* Pros, Indians; *Baltimore:* Colts; *Boston:* Bullfrogs, Yanks; *Brooklyn:* Lions, Dodgers, Tigers; *Buffalo:* All-Americans, Bisons[1], Rangers; *Canton:* Bulldogs; *Chicago:* Tigers; *Cincinnati:* Celts, Reds; *Cleveland:* Tigers, Indians[2], Bulldogs[3]; *Columbus:* Panhandles, Tigers; *Dallas:* Texans; *Dayton:* Triangles; *Detroit:* Heralds, Panthers, Wolverines; *Duluth:* Kelleys, Eskimoes; *Evansville:* Crimson Giants; *Frankford:* Yellow Jackets; *Hammond:* Pros; *Hartford:* Blues; *Kansas City:* Blues, Cowboys; *Kenosha:* Maroons; *Los Angeles:* Buccaneers; *Louisville:* Brecks, Colonels; *Marion:* Oorang Indians; *Milwaukee:* Badgers; *Minneapolis:* Marines, Red Jackets; *Muncie:* Flyers; *New York:* Giants, Yankees[4], Bulldogs; *Newark:* Tornadoes; *Orange:* Tornadoes; *Pottsville:* Maroons; *Providence:* Steam Rollers; *Racine:* Legion, Tornadoes; *Rochester:* Jeffersons; *Rock Island:* Independents; *Staten Island:* Stapletons; *St Louis:* All-Stars, Gunners; *Toledo:* Maroons; *Tanawanda:* Kardex[5]; *Washington:* Senators.

1 Bisons founded 1924, folded 1925, revived 1927, folded 1928, revived 1929, then folded; 2 Indians active twice: 1921 and 1923; 3 Bulldogs active twice: 1924–25 and 1927; 4 Yankees active twice: 1927–28 and 1950–51; 5 also known as Lumbermen.

TEAM OF THE CENTURY

————•◦•————

Composition of Australian cricket's Team of the Century, a joint initiative of the Australian Cricket Board and the Australian Cricketers' Association, was announced on 18 January 2000: Arthur Morris, Bill Ponsford, Sir Donald Bradman (captain), Greg Chappell, Neil Harvey, Keith Miller, Ian Healy, Ray Lindwall, Shane Warne, Dennis Lillee, Bill O'Reilly, Allan Border (12th man). The team was chosen from all those who had represented Australia during the twentieth century after polling twenty past and present players and pundits.

*Ensure the piece of paper you use is square.*

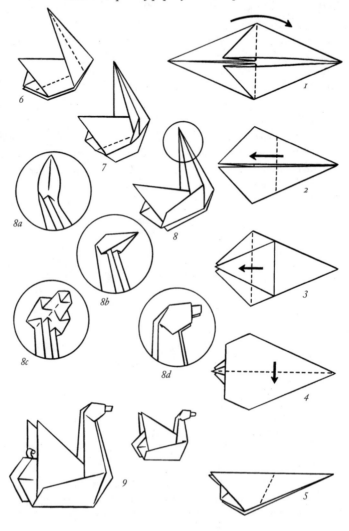

*bildungsroman* . . . . . . . . . . . . . novel dealing with protagonist's early development or education.

*entwicklungsroman* . . . . . . . . . . . . . novel dealing with protagonist's development from childhood to maturity.

## ORIGINS OF OZ

The derivation of Oz, the fantasy land ruled by a Wonderful Wizard from Emerald Citycreated by New York journalist Lyman Frank Baum (1856–1919), has been variously explained by biographers:

1 Baum modified the name from the kingdom of Uz, Job's homeland.
2 Baum, delighted in the exhalations of 'Oohs' and 'Ahs' from his children, respelt them.
3 Baum was inspired by the pen name, 'Boz', of his hero Charles Dickens.
4 Baum, in an interview with the *St Louis Despatch*, said that the name was derived from the drawer of a three-tier filing cabinet labelled 'O-Z'.
5 Baum's work is an allegorical treatment of the *fin de siècle* conflict between the gold standard and bimetallism. Oz comes from the abbreviation of ounce, in which both gold and silver are traded; the Yellow Brick Road is said to symbolise the gold standard, the witch's silver shoes to represent silver coinage, and the Cowardly Lion is purportedly William Jennings Bryan, unsuccessful candidate in the 1896 presidential election, whose Cross of Gold speech is the dispute's most famous cultural artefact.

## SPEEDS OF LIGHT

*Kilometres per second*
Through air 298,051 km/s; through ice 227,200 km/s;
through glass 174,400 km/s; through diamond 123,200 km/s.

*What Cato did and Addison approved/Cannot be wrong.*
In 1737 Grub Street hack Eustace Budgell leapt into the Thames, his pockets weighted with stones. Of the unfinished couplet, A. Alvarez remarked: 'His muse was unfaithful even in death.'

*And so I leave this world, where the heart must either break or turn to lead.*
Nicolas-Sebastien Chamfort, French playwright and cynic, died of wounds from a suicide attempt while imprisoned during the Terror, 1794.

*I have gone to the Yarra. It is best for all.*
Dick Wardill, the first batsman to score a century in Australian first-class cricket history, cast himself into the Yarra river after being exposed as an embezzler, 17 August 1873.

*They tried to get me—I got them first!*
Poet Vachel Lindsay, who took his life by drinking Lysol on 4 December 1931.

*To my friends. My work is done. Why wait? G. E*
George Eastman, founder of Kodak and aged seventy-seven, shot himself through the heart on 14 March 1932, after a period of ill-health.

*All fled—all done, so lift me on the pyre;/The feast is over, and the lamps expire.*
Robert E. Howard, creator of comic-strip figure *Conan the Barbarian*, who shot himself in the head on 11 June 1936.

*I feel certain that I'm going mad again. I feel we can't go through another of those terrible times. And I shan't recover this time. I begin to hear voices.*
Novelist Virginia Woolf, who drowned herself, 28 March 1941.

*Such insomnia. I had to commit suicide.*
Actor Herman Bing, star of *Dinner at Eight* and *The Great Ziegfeld*, shot himself in the heart on 10 January 1948.

*I am sickened by all this. Not words. Action. I shall write no more.*
Italian novelist Cesare Pavese, who swallowed twelve sachets of sleeping pills, 27 August 1950.

*Dear World, I am leaving you because I am bored. I feel I have lived long enough. I am leaving you with your worries in this sweet cesspool—good luck.*
Russian-born British actor George Sanders overdosed on barbiturates, 25 April 1972. Kenneth Anger summarised his life as 'four wives and seven psychiatrists'.

*I must end it. There's no hope left. I'll be at peace. No one had anything to do with this. My decision totally.*
Comedian and actor Freddie Prinze, star of *Chico and the Man*, shot himself 29 January 1977.

*I can't live any longer with my nerves.*
Actress Jean Seaberg, star of *Breathless* and *Lilith*, overdosed on barbiturates, 1 September 1979.

*Frances and Courtney, I'll be at your altar. Please keep going Courtney, for Frances, for her life will be so much happier without me. I LOVE YOU. I LOVE YOU.*
Kurt Cobain, lead singer of Nirvana, shot himself in the head, 8 April 1994.

*Don't feel sorry for me. I've had a great life, great friends. Please think of the real O.J. and not this lost person. Thanks for making my life special. I hope I helped yours. Peace and love, O.J.*
Suicide note drafted but unused by O. J. Simpson.

## AUSTRALIAN BIG THINGS

NEW SOUTH WALES: *Big Avocado*, Byron Bay; *Big Banana*, Coffs Harbour; *Big Bottle*, Mangrove Mountain; *Big Bull*, Wauchope; *Big Cheese*, Bega; *Big Guitar*, Tamworth; *Big Merino*, Goulburn; *Big Orange*, Tenterfield; *Big Oyster*, Taree; *Big Potato*, Robertson; *Big Prawn*, Ballina; *Big Rock*, Barrington Tops; *Big Trout*, Adaminaby.

QUEENSLAND: *Big Cow*, *Big Macadamia* and *Big Pineapple*, Nambour; *Big Peanut*, Kingaroy.

SOUTH AUSTRALIA: *Big Rocking Horse*, Gumeracha.

VICTORIA: *Big Lobster*, Kingston; *Big Ned Kelly*, Glenrowan.

The most consistently successful sharemarket investor of the postwar period, Warren Buffett, obeys the following maxims, as documented in Robert Hagstrom's *The Warren Buffett Way* (1994):

Step One: *Turn off the stock market*
'Remember that the stockmarket is a manic depressive...wildly excited...and at other times unreasonably depressed.'

Step Two: *Don't worry about the economy*
'Buffett dedicates no time or energy analysing the economy.'

Step Three: *Buy a business, not a stock*
'You cannot make an intelligent guess about the future of your business unless you understand how it makes money.'

Step Four: *Manage a portfolio of businesses*
'It is wrong to assume that if you are not buying and selling, you are not making progress...It is too difficult to make hundreds of smart decisions in a lifetime.'

## DAMPER WHEN CAMPING

3 cups of self-raising flour, 2 teaspoons salt, 1 cup of water.
Find several green sticks. Mix ingredients together. Press the dough around one end of stick to form an oblong-like shape (rather like a large hot dog). Ensure other end of stick is free of dough, to use as a handle. Place on fire's hot coals. Turn several times during cooking, approx. 20–30 minutes. Eat hot with butter and jam. Serves 6.

## THE GANG OF FOUR

Jiang Qing—Zhang Chunqiao—Yao Wenyuan—Wang Hongwen

**A**: found in liver, eggs, yellow and green vegetables. Essential for normal growth of skeleton and good vision. Also known as retinol.

**B**: comes in several varieties, including: B1 (thiamine), found in yeast and pork, contributes to musculature and mental agility; B2 (riboflavin), found in dairy products, eggs and kidneys, is important for skin, eyes and digestion; B3 (niacin), helps release energy from carbohydrates and fats; B12 (cobalamin), occurring in animal foods but not in vegetables and thus sometimes lacking in a vegetarian diet, is vital to the health of the nervous system, and improves red blood cell count.

**C**: found in citrus fruits and vegetables, especially potatoes, maintains bones and teeth and aids the healing process. Also known as ascorbic acid.

**D**: not a vitamin *per se*, as the best source is not a food but sunshine: also helps maintain bones. Also known as calciferol.

**E**: found in most foods, but especially vegetable oils and grains. Believed to prevent sterility.

**K**: comes in several varieties, including: K1 (phytonadione), K2 (the menaquinones) and K3 (menadione). Produced within the body, they counteract anticoagulants and thus aid clotting.

Water soluble vitamins: B, C. Fat soluble vitamins: A, D, E, K.
Result of deficiencies: A—night blindness; B1—beriberi; B3—pellagra; C—scurvy; D—rickets.

## OHM'S LAW

This law states that electrical current is produced according to the formula $I = V/R$, where $I$ is the amperage (current), $V$ is the voltage (variations in charge at different points in conductor) and $R$ is the resistance.

| *Battle* | *War, Date* | *Victorious Admiral, Flagship* | *Defeated Admiral, Flagship* |
| --- | --- | --- | --- |
| SPANISH ARMADA | Spanish Wars, July 1588 | Lord Howard of Effingham (England), *Ark Royal*[1] | Duke of Medina Sidonia (Spain), *San Martin* |
| THE DOWNS | Dutch–Spanish War, September 1639 | Marten Tromp (Holland), *Amelia* | General Don Antonio d'Oquendo (Spain/Portugal), *Santiago* |
| THE FOUR DAYS' BATTLE | 2nd Anglo-Dutch War, June 1666 | Michel de Ruyter (Holland), *Zeven Provincian* | Duke of Albemarle (England), *Royal Charles* |
| QUIBERON BAY | Seven Years' War, November 1759 | Sir Edward Hawke (Britain), *Royal George* | Marshal de Conflans (France), *Soleil Royal* |
| CHESAPEAKE BAY | American War of Independence, September 1781 | Comte de Grasse (France), *Ville de Paris* | Thomas Graves (Britain), *London* |
| GLORIOUS FIRST OF JUNE | Revolutionary, Wars, June 1794 | Lord Howe (Britain), *Queen Charlotte* | Louis Villaret de Joyeuse (France), *Montagne* |
| THE NILE | Napoleonic Wars, August 1798 | Horatio Nelson (Britain), *Vanguard* | Comte de Brueys d'Aigailliers* (France), *L'Orient* |

| | | | |
|---|---|---|---|
| COPENHAGEN | British–Danish Crisis, April 1801[2] | Horatio Nelson (Britain), *Elephant* | J. Olfert Fischer (Denmark), *Dannebrog* |
| TRAFALGAR | Napoleonic Wars, November 1805 | Horatio Nelson*, *Victory* | Pierre-Charles Jean-Baptiste-Sylvestre de Villeneuve[3], *Bucentaure* |
| MOBILE | American Civil War, July 1864 | David Farragut (Federals), *Hartford* | Franklin Buchanan (Confederates), *Tennessee* |
| TSUSHIMA STRAITS | Russo-Japanese War, May 1905 | Heimachoro Togo (Japan), *Mikasa* | Zinovii Rozhdestvenskii[4] (Russia), *Suvaroff* |
| JUTLAND[5] | World War I, May 1916 | Sir John Jellicoe (Britain), *Iron Duke* | Reinhard von Scheer (Germany), *Friedrich der Grosse* |
| MIDWAY | World War II, June 1942 | Raymond Spruance & Frank Fletcher (USA), *Enterprise* (Spruance) & *Yorktown* (Fletcher) | Chuichi Nagumo (Japan), *Akagi* |
| LEYTE GULF | World War II, August 1944 | Bill Halsey (USA), *New Jersey* | Takeo Kurita (Japan)[6], *Yamato* |

* Killed; 1 Sold to the Crown by Sir Walter Raleigh; 2 Not part of declared war, but to prevent Danish fleet aligning itself with Napoleon after Russia's Emperor Paul I struck an alliance with Danes, Swedes and Prussians; 3 Made prisoner of the British, then repatriated. In April 1806 he stabbed himself six times in the heart rather than face Napoleon. 4 Injured and relieved during battle by Nikolai Nebagatov; 5 Outcome disputed: Germans inflicted greater casualties, British left in control of sea; 6 Japanese forces divided into three with Kurita's the largest: the other detachments were commanded by Jisaburo Ozawa (*Zuikaku*) and Shoji Nishimura (*Fuso*)/Kiyohide Shima (*Nachi*).

*argentocracy* . . . . . . . . . . . . . . . . . . . . . . . . . . . . . . . ruled by money
*aristarchy* . . . . . . . . . . . . . . . . . . . . . . . . . ruled by the most qualified
*boobocracy* . . . . . . . . . . . . . . . . . . . . . . . . . . . . . . . . ruled by fools
*capelocracy* . . . . . . . . . . . . . . . . . . . . . . . . . . ruled by shopkeepers
*ergatocracy* . . . . . . . . . . . . . . . . . . . . . . . . . . ruled by the workers
*gerontocracy* . . . . . . . . . . . . . . . . . . . . . . . . . . . . ruled by the old
*gynarchy* . . . . . . . . . . . . . . . . . . . . . . . . . . . . . . . ruled by women
*hagiarchy* . . . . . . . . . . . . . . . . . . . . . . . . . ruled by religious types
*iatrarchy* . . . . . . . . . . . . . . . . . . . . . . . . . . . . ruled by physicians
*isocracy* . . . . . . . . . . . . . . . . . . . . . . . . . where all have equal power
*kakistocracy* . . . . . . . . . . . . . . . . . . . . . . . . . . . ruled by the worst
*neocracy* . . . . . . . . . . . . . . . . . . . . . . . . . ruled by the inexperienced
*ochlocracy* . . . . . . . . . . . . . . . . . . . . . . . . . . . . . ruled by the mob
*pornocracy* . . . . . . . . . . . . . . . . . . . . . . . . . . ruled by prostitutes
*ptochocracy* . . . . . . . . . . . . . . . . . . . . . . . . . . . ruled by the poor
*squirearchy* . . . . . . . . . . . . . . . . . . . . . . . . ruled by landed gentry
*statocracy* . . . . . . . . . . . . . . . . . . . . . . . . . . . ruled by the military
*uxorarchy* . . . . . . . . . . . . . . . . . . . . . . . . . . . . . . . ruled by wives

## WHY THE ANTARCTIC IS COLDER THAN THE ARCTIC

At neither the North nor South Pole does the sun rise more than 23.5 degrees above the horizon, and most of the light cast is reflected by the bright white surface. But the South Pole is the colder because of its height: it reposes on top of a very thick ice sheet, which itself sits on a continent, rising as much as 3000 metres above sea level. The North Pole, by contrast, rests in the middle of the Arctic Ocean, where the surface of floating ice rides only a foot or so above the surrounding sea. The Arctic Ocean also preserves heat, warming the atmosphere in winter, and drawing heat from it in summer.

Ayer's Cherry Pectoral, Bonnington's Irish Moss, Brown's Vermifuge Comfits, Brown's Household Panacea, Carney's Common Sense Cure, Derbeyshire's Patent Embrocation for Preventing Sea-Sickness, De Witt's Eclectic Cure, Dill's Balm of Life, Dr Chamlee Cancer Cure, Classe's Great Penetrating Liniment, Dr Grinrod's Remedy for Spasms, Dr J. Collis Brown's Chlorodyne, Dr Seth Arnold's Cough Killer, Eli Lilly Camphorated Tincture of Opium Tablets, Ford's Balsam of Horehound, Ingham's Vegetable Expectorant Nervine Pain Extractor, Jayne's Expectorant, Keating's Cough Lozenges, McMunn's Elixir of Opium, Piso's Cure for Consumption, Squibb's Diarrhoea Mixture, Steward's Mother's Blessing, Street's Infant Quietness, Sweet Rest for Children, Thomas's Electric Oil, Thompson's Soothing Syrup for Baby, Trafton's Balm of Life, Venice Treacle, Walker's Pain Destroyer, Winslow's Soothing Syrup, Perry Davis Pain Killer, Wistar's Balsam of Wild Cherry.

## THE THREE INVESTIGATORS

Jupiter Jones—Pete Crenshaw—Bob Andrews

## HOW TO MEASURE A CHILD'S FEET FOR SHOES

1 Cut two thin strips of cardboard longer than the feet.
2 Stand the child on them with one bare foot on each strip.
3 Draw marks on the cardboard strip at the back of the heel and the longest toe of the foot.
4 Mark the strips 'left' and 'right', and cut the cardboard at those marks.
5 Place a strip in each shoe, so that the ends touch the toes of the shoes. If the shoe is the correct length, there should be about half an inch (1.3cm) of 'growing gap' between the end of the strip and the heel end of the shoe.

*O sancta simplicitas! (O holy simplicity!)*
John Huss (c. 1372–1415), being burned at the stake for heresy and seeing a peasant approaching with a bundle of sticks.

*Ich kann nicht anders. (I can do no other.)*
Martin Luther (1483–1546), asked to recant at Diet of Worms, 18 April 1521.

*Eppur si muove. (But it does move.)*
Galileo Galilei (1564–1642) after his recantation from stating that the Earth moves round the Sun, in 1632.

*I have not yet begun to fight.*
Admiral John Paul Jones (1747–1792) during the *Bonhomme Richard*'s engagement with HMS *Serapis*, on being asked whether he was lowering his flag off Farnborough Head, 23 September 1779.

*Damn the torpedoes! Full steam ahead!*
Admiral David Glasgow Farragut, at the Battle of Mobile Bay, 5 August 1864. ('Torpedoes' then meant mines.)

*God damn you all: I told you so.*
A suggestion by H. G. Wells (1866–1946) for his own epitaph.

*I came through and I shall return.*
General Douglas MacArthur (1880–1964) on reaching Australia, 20 March 1942, from the Philippines.

*Nuts!*
General Anthony McAuliffe (1898–1975), replying to Germans who sought his surrender at Bastogne, Belgium, 22 December 1944.

*I will return and I will be millions.*
Inscription on the tomb of Eva Peron (1919–1952), Buenos Aires, Argentina.

| Michael Howe | beaten to death, Tasmania | 1818 |
| Musquito | hanged, Tasmania | 1825 |
| Matthew Brady | hanged, Tasmania | 1826 |
| Jack Donohue | shot, New South Wales | 1830 |
| Edward Davis | hanged, New South Wales | 1841 |
| Frank Gardiner | jailed, New South Wales | 1864/ exiled 1874 |
| Dan Morgan | shot, Victoria | 1865 |
| Ben Hall | shot, New South Wales | 1865 |
| John Gilbert | shot, New South Wales | 1865 |
| Thomas Clarke/ John Clarke | hanged, New South Wales | 1867 |
| Frederick Ward[1] | shot, New South Wales | 1870 |
| Andrew George Scott[2] | hanged, Victoria | 1879 |
| Ned Kelly | hanged, Victoria | 1880 |
| Jimmy Governor | hanged, New South Wales | 1901 |

1 Captain Thunderbolt 2 Captain Moonlight

## GERMAN CHANCELLORS

| 1949–63 | Konrad Adenauer | Christian Democrats |
| 1963–66 | Ludwig Erhard | Christian Democrats |
| 1966–69 | Kurt Georg Kiesinger | Christian Democrats |
| 1969–74 | Willy Brandt | Social Democrats |
| 1974–82 | Helmut Schmidt | Social Democrats |
| 1982–98 | Helmut Kohl | Christian Democrats |
| 1998– | Gerhard Schroder | Social Democrats |

'Americans of all ages, all conditions and all dispositions constantly form associations.' *Alexis de Tocqueville in* Democracy in America *(1840). The US contains about 100,000 known associations and clubs; seven in ten Americans belong to at least one. They include:*

*Benevolent and Loyal Order of Pessimists.* Founded 1975. Purpose: Why bother stating it? Meets annually on 15 April, the anniversary of the sinking of the *Titanic.* President recently quoted as saying: 'I'm pessimistic about doomsday.' Abbreviation: BLOOP. Motto: 'No matter what it is, don't count on it.'

*International Association of Professional Bureaucrats.* Founded 1968. Purpose: 'Promotes excellence in dynamic inaction, orbital dialoguing and creative non-responsiveness'. Abbreviation: INAPROBU. Motto: 'When in doubt, mumble.'

*National Organisation Taunting Safety and Fairness Everywhere.* Founded 1982. Purpose: Formed as a response to the American obsession with safety and equity by a former air traffic controller who suggested that airliners avoid crashes by taxiing everywhere. Abbreviation: NOTSAFE. Motto: 'You can't be too careful.'

*Procrastinators Club of America.* Founded 1956. Purpose: Still seeking to elect first president. Made protest against war of 1812 in 1967. Abbreviation: Undecided. Motto: 'We're behind you all the way.'

*Society for Basic Irreproducible Research.* Founded 1956. Purpose: 'To blunt the cutting edge of scientific research'. Publishes such papers as 'Calculating the Velocity of Darkness and Its Possible Relevance to Lawn Maintenance', 'Utilization of the Pencil and Ruler Protocol in Drug Study Design' and 'The Use of Patient Self-Directed Sham Liposuction Procedures as a Treatment for Anorexia Nervosa'.

*Society for the Preservation and Enhancement of the Recognition of Millard Fillmore, Last of the Whigs.* Founded 1975. Purpose: 'To defend global standards of mediocrity'. Abbreviation: SPERMFLOW. Motto: *E pluribus mediocritum.*

In 1999, to mark the coming of a new millennium, the Modern Library polled a group of judges and surveyed readers about the outstanding novels of the twentieth century.

Judges chose:

1. *Ulysses* by James Joyce
2. *The Great Gatsby* by F. Scott Fitzgerald
3. *A Portrait of the Artist* by James Joyce
4. *Lolita* by Vladimir Nabokov
5. *Brave New World* by Aldous Huxley
6. *The Sound and the Fury* by William Faulkner
7. *Catch-22* by Joseph Heller
8. *Darkness at Noon* by Arthur Koestler
9. *Sons and Lovers* by D. H. Lawrence
10. *The Grapes of Wrath* by John Steinbeck

Readers chose:

1. *Atlas Shrugged* by Ayn Rand
2. *The Fountainhead* by Ayn Rand
3. *Battlefield Earth* by L. Ron Hubbard
4. *The Lord of the Rings* by J. R. R. Tolkien
5. *To Kill a Mockingbird* by Harper Lee
6. *1984* by George Orwell
7. *Anthem* by Ayn Rand
8. *We the Living* by Ayn Rand
9. *Mission Earth* by L. Ron Hubbard
10. *Fear* by L. Ron Hubbard

## THE SECRET SEVEN

Peter—Jack—Barbara—George—Pam—
Colin—Janet—Scamper (the dog)

*Australia* All Ordinaries; *Austria* ATX; *Belgium* Bel 20; *Britain* FTSE100; *Canada* Toronto Composite; *Denmark* KBX; France CAC40; *Germany* DAX; *Italy* BCI; *Japan* Nikkei 225; *Netherlands* AEX; *Spain* Madrid SE; *Sweden* Affarsviden Gen; *Switzerland* Swiss Market; *United States* Dow-Jones Industrial Average.

## TRAITOR BROADCASTERS

*Axis Sally* Mildred Gillars (1900–1988), Germany;
Rita Zucca (1912–), Italy

*The BBC Spy* Johannes Dronkers (1896–1942), Germany*

*Lord Haw-Haw* William Joyce (1906–1946), Germany

*Tokyo Rose* Iva Ikuko Togori D'Aquino (1916–), Japan

---

* Dutch Nazi hanged after seeking to infiltrate the BBC.

## HOW ORGANISMS ASSOCIATE

*Parasitism:* relationship between two species in which one (the parasite) benefits at the expense of another species (the host).

*Commensalism:* relationship between two species in which one benefits while the other neither benefits nor is harmed.

*Mutualism:* relationship between two species in which both species benefit.

*Symbiosis:* relationship between two species in which either commensalism or mutualism results.

Festivals honouring the mother figure date back to pre-Christian times: the Greeks celebrated a day in spring to honour the mother of the gods, Rhea. The oldest surviving custom is Mothering Sunday, traditionally a day in the UK when children working as domestic servants were free to visit mother and family, now marked on the fourth Sunday in Lent. Its origins lie in the sixteenth century, when it was important to return to one's home or 'mother' church once a year. As they threaded country lanes, children would pick flowers to take to church or give to their mother as a small gift.

The first Mother's Day was 10 May 1908 in Grafton, West Virginia, USA. It consisted of a service in praise of motherhood at Andrews Methodist Sunday school, attended by 407 children and their mothers; the text was John 19:26–27 (Christ's parting words to his mother and a disciple). It was instigated by spinster schoolteacher, Anna Jarvis (1864–1948), still bereft at the death of her mother, a veteran Sunday school teacher, three years earlier. Jarvis's correspondence in favour of national recognition of Mother's Day became so vigorous and voluminous that six years later President Woodrow Wilson designated the second Sunday in May as an official occasion for honouring mothers. Jarvis bemoaned the secular consumerism that came to overshadow her idea; she died a recluse, embittered by her failure as a litigant against companies seeking to exploit Mother's Day for commercial ends.

The first Father's Day was 10 June 1910 in Spokane, Washington. It too was designed as a church ceremony and was the idea of Sonora Smart Dodd (1882–1978), inspired by her father, a Civil War veteran who had raised six children after his wife's death in 1898. It was not until 1972, however, that President Richard Nixon signed a proclamation establishing Father's Day in the national calendar on the third Sunday in June, a date which is also followed by the UK. In Australia, however, Father's Day occurs in September.

Also marked in the US are Grandparents' Day (since 1978 the Sunday after Labor Day) and Mother-in-Laws' Day (since 1981 the fourth Sunday in October).

Oceans. . . . . . . . . . . . . . . . . . . . . . . . . . . . . . . . . 97.3 per cent
Glaciers/polar ice . . . . . . . . . . . . . . . . . . . . . . . . . . 2.1 per cent
Underground aquifers. . . . . . . . . . . . . . . . . . . . . . . . 0.6 per cent
Lakes and rivers . . . . . . . . . . . . . . . . . . . . . . . . . . . 0.01 per cent
Atmosphere . . . . . . . . . . . . . . . . . . . . . . . . . . . . . 0.001 per cent

# MARK TWAIN

Raised on the banks of the Mississippi near Hannibal, Missouri, Samuel Langhorne Clemens (1835–1910) fulfilled a youthful ambition of becoming a licensed riverboat pilot at the age of twenty-four. His career was curtailed by the Civil War, but was perpetuated in his chosen *nom de plume*. The expression 'mark twain' was used by riverboat crewmen to denote water depth of two fathoms (12ft)—'twain' is an archaic word for two, from the Middle English 'twayn'. 'It has a richness about it,' he explained. 'It was always a pleasant sound for a pilot to hear on a dark night; it meant safe water.'

Clemens wasn't the first to make this observation. He only took the pseudonym in January 1863 when another riverboat captain turned writer who had used it, Isaiah Sellers, died. In *Mark Twain: A Biography* (1912), Albert Bigelow Paine described the author's reasoning—and reservations: 'Sellers would never need it again. Clemens decided he would give it a new meaning and new association in this far-away land...He did not then mention that Captain Isaiah Sellers had used and dropped the name. He was ashamed of his part in that episode, and the offence was still too recent for confession.' But the name's appearance on his first successful comic tale, 'The Celebrated Jumping Frog of Calaveras County' (1865), and on his first bestselling book of travel writings, *Innocents Abroad* (1867), made it his own. Paine judged 'Mark Twain' fundamental to Clemens' success: 'the greatest *nom de plume* ever chosen', it became 'a name exactly in accord with the man, his work, and his career'.

| No. in harmonic series | 1 | 2 | 3 | 4 | 5 | 6 | 7 | 8 | 9 | etc |
|---|---|---|---|---|---|---|---|---|---|---|
| degree in which string or air column is vibrating | whole | $1/2$ | $1/3$ | $1/4$ | $1/5$ | $1/6$ | $1/7$ | $1/8$ | $1/9$ | etc |

octave   perfect fifth   perfect fourth   etc

The harmonic series is the set of tones, or harmonics, produced from a vibrating string or wind through a tubular device, and whether this is vibrating through its whole length or only a part. Vibration of the whole length results in the lowest tone, also known as the fundamental. The other tones are called the upper partials and occur at fixed intervals above the fundamental.

CATCHPHRASES FROM 'THE GOON SHOW'

*No more curried eggs for me!* Major Denis Bloodnok *
*Ar-Low!* Eccles †
*Pauses for audience applause. Not a sausage. You rotten swine, you.* Bluebottle *
*You can't get the wood, you know.* Henry Crun *
*We'll all be murdered in our beds.* Minnie Bannister †
*You silly twisted boy, you.* Hercules Grytpype-Thynne *
*Owwww!* Count Jim Moriarty †
*Hello, Jim.* Jim Spriggs †
*He's fallen in the water.* Little Jim †
*Oooh, I could spit!* Lew *
*Hello, mate.* William Cobblers *
*Hello, folks. Where's my megaphone?* Neddy Seagoon ^

* Played by Peter Sellers. † Played by Spike Milligan.
^ Played by Harry Secombe.

SIGNS OF THE ZODIAC

| SYMBOL & SIGN | DATES | ASPECTS | REPRESENTATIVES |
|---|---|---|---|
| | | *Element, Quality, Ruler, Mode, Motto* | *Art, Literature, Music, Politics, Film, Thought* |
| Aries: Ram ♈ | 21 March – 20 April | Fire, Cardinal, Mars, Intuition, *I am* | da Vinci, Beckett, Bach, Kohl, Chaplin, Descartes |
| Taurus: Bull ♉ | 21 April – 21 May | Earth, Fixed, Venus, Sensation, *I have* | Braques, Shakespeare, Ellington, Marx, Astaire, Kant |
| Gemini: Twins ♊ | 22 May – 21 June | Air, Mutable, Mercury, Thought, *I communicate* | Gauguin, Conan Doyle, Davis (M), Victoria, Wayne, Emerson |
| Cancer: Crab ♋ | 22 June – 23 July | Water, Cardinal, Moon, Feeling, *I feel* | Rembrandt, Orwell, Guthrie, Mandela, Streep, Leibniz |
| Leo: Lion ♌ | 24 July – 23 August | Fire, Fixed, Sun, Intuition, *I create* | Reynolds, Chandler, Madonna, Napoleon, de Niro, Jung |
| Virgo: Virgin ♍ | 24 August – 23 September | Earth, Mutable, Mercury, Sensation, *I serve* | David, Shelley (M), Basie, Deng, Garbo, Koestler |

| SYMBOL & SIGN | DATES | ASPECTS<br>*Element, Quality, Ruler, Mode, Motto* | REPRESENTATIVES<br>*Art, Literature, Music, Politics, Film, Thought* |
|---|---|---|---|
| ♎ Libra:<br>Scales | 24 September –<br>22 October | Air, Cardinal, Venus,<br>Thought, *I weigh* | Rothko, Faulkner, Pavarotti,<br>Gandhi, Bardot, Diderot |
| ♏ Scorpio:<br>Scorpion | 23 October –<br>22 November | Water, Fixed, Pluto,<br>Feeling, *I control* | Picasso, Keats, Paderewski,<br>Roosevelt (T), Kelly, Erasmus |
| ♐ Sagittarius:<br>Archer | 23 November –<br>22 December | Fire, Mutable, Jupiter,<br>Intuition, *I philosophise* | Toulouse-Lautrec, Twain,<br>Beethoven, Churchill, Disney,<br>Santayana |
| ♑ Capricorn:<br>Goat | 23 December –<br>20 January | Earth, Cardinal, Saturn,<br>Sensation, *I master* | Matisse, Kipling, Beefheart (Captain),<br>Mao, Hopkins, Spinoza |
| ♒ Aquarius:<br>Water Bearer | 21 January –<br>19 February | Air, Fixed, Uranus,<br>Thought, *I universalise* | Pollock, Dickens, Mozart, Lincoln,<br>Humphries, Ramakrishna |
| ✴ Pisces:<br>The Fish | 20 February –<br>20 March | Water, Mutable, Neptune,<br>Feeling, *I believe* | Michelangelo, Nin, Cobain,<br>Gorbachev, Taylor (E), Einstein |

The Arctic produces only 7 per cent of the world's icebergs, and they are generally far smaller than those to the south. In the Antarctic, iceberg names are derived from the Antarctic quadrant in which they are first detected, the quadrants dividing in the following manner: A: 0–90°W (Bellinghausen/Weddell Sea); B: 90°W–180° (Amundsen/Eastern Ross Sea); C: 180°–90°E (Western Ross Sea/Wilkesland); D: 90°E – 0° (Amery/Eastern Weddell Sea).

## ROMAN EXCLAMATIONS

*mehercule!* By Hercules!
*pro di immortales!* By the Gods!
*ecastor!* By Castor!
*edepol!* By Pollux!
*quaevis numina!* By whatever Gods you please!
(a favourite of Ovid's)

## SANTA'S REINDEER

*A Visit from St Nicholas* (1823) by Clement Clarke Moore (1779–1863), the ur-text of most modern Christmas ritual, lists eight reindeer (in alphabetical order): Blitzen, Comet, Cupid, Dancer, Dasher, Donder, Prancer and Vixen. Donder became Donner in Ken Darby's musical score, *'Twas the Night before Christmas* (1954).

The most famous, however, was the braindeer of Robert L. May, a copywriter at retail giant Montgomery Ward who cast red-nosed Rudolph in a promotional ballad for Christmas 1939. Two and a half million copies of the story were sold, and another three million when it was reissued seven years later. The sales of the song 'Rudolph the Red-Nosed Reindeer' (1949) by Johnny Marks and first recorded by Gene Autry have since exceeded 160 million.

Baptism—Penance—Holy Eucharist—Confirmation—Holy Order—
Matrimony—Extreme Unction

PI

Pi (π), the sixteenth letter of the Greek alphabet, denotes an irrational number which is the ratio of the circumference of a circle to its diameter. Mathematical calculations of its value began in about 2000 B.C., the so-called Rhind papyrus figuring it at 3.16045. Archimedes had sharpened this to 3.1418 by 250 B.C, Ptolemy to 3.14166 by 150, the remarkable Chinese mathematician Tsu Ch'ung Chi to 3.141592920 (or 355/113) by A.D. 480. Sir Isaac Newton calculated π correctly to sixteen decimal places in 1665, and it had been resolved using manual means to 620 decimal places shortly after World War II. Calculators and computers have subsequently turned its solution into an exhibition of pedantry. Twenty years ago, π had been correctly resolved to 10 million places; Japanese mathematicians Kanada and Takahashi have since used a Hitachi SR8000 to calculate it to 206,158,430,000 places. This is π to 600 places:

3.1415926535 8979323846 2643383279 5028841971 6939937510
5820974944 5923078164 0628620899 8628034825 3421170679
8214808651 3282306647 0938446095 5058223172 5359408128
4811174502 8410270193 8521105559 6446229489 5493038196
4428810975 6659334461 2847564823 3786783165 2712019091
4564856692 3460348610 4543266482 1339360726 0249141273
7245870066 0631558817 4881520920 9628292540 9171536436
7892590360 0113305305 4882046652 1384146951 9415116094
3305727036 5759591953 0921861173 8193261179 3105118548
0744623799 6274956735 1885752724 8912279381 8301194912
9833673362 4406566430 8602139494 6395224737 1907021798
6094370277 0539217176 2931767523 8467481846 7669405132

*Waverley Cemetery in the Sydney suburb of Bronte opened in 1877.
Covering over sixteen hectares (41 acres), it contains graves of the following
notable Australians:*

| | |
|---|---|
| Daniel Henry Deniehey (1822–1865) | Editor, orator, political firebrand. |
| Fanny Durack (1889–1956) | Olympic swimming gold medallist. |
| Michael Dwyer (1772–1882) | Irish incendiary known as the 'Wicklow Chieftain'. |
| Sir Francis Forbes (1784–1841) | First Chief Justice of New South Wales. |
| Lawrence Hargrave (1850–1915) | Pioneer aviator |
| Lt. Col. George Johnston (1764–1823) | First Fleet veteran court-martialled for arresting Governor Bligh during the Rum Rebellion. |
| Henry Kendall (1839–1882) | Poet, 'Muse of Australia'. |
| Henry Lawson (1867–1922) | Author, poet, bushman. |
| Dorothea Mackellar (1885–1968) | Poet, 'My Country'. |
| Sir James Martin (1820–1886) | Twice NSW Premier, gave name to Martin Place. |
| Maj.-Gen. John Soame Richardson (1836–1896) | Commandant NSW Military Forces 1871–92. |
| Harry Rickards (1845–1911) | Thespian, impresario. |
| Victor Trumper (1877–1915) | Revered cricketer. |

TEMPERATURE CONVERSION

To obtain Celsius from Fahrenheit: (°F − 32) ÷ 1.8

To obtain Fahrenheit from Celsius: (°C × 1.8) + 32

The magnitude of earthquakes has since 1935 been measured on the Richter scale, a mathematical tool invented by Charles F. Richter of the California Institute of Technology based on a logarithm of the amplitude of waves recorded by seismographs, adjusted for the distance of measuring instruments from the epicentre. An older, more subjective, but sometimes more meaningful scale, named for the Italian geologist who devised it in 1902, Giuseppe Mercalli, expresses an earthquake's intensity by observation:

I    Not felt at all.

II    Felt only by a few individuals, indoors and at rest, usually on upper floors of tall buildings.

III    Felt indoors by many persons, but not necessarily recognised as an earthquake. Chandeliers and hanging plants swing.

IV    Felt both indoors and out. Feels like the vibration caused by a heavy truck or train passing. Windows rattle.

V    Strong enough to awaken sleeping persons. Small objects knocked off shelves. Beverages may splash out of cups or glasses on tables.

VI    Perceptible to everyone. May cause public fright. Pictures fall off walls. Weak masonry cracks. Some plaster may fall from ceilings.

VII    Difficult to stand upright. Ornamental masonry falls from buildings. Waves may be seen in ponds and swimming pools.

VIII    Mass panic may occur. Chimneys, smoke stacks and water towers may lean and fall. Unsecured frame houses slide off foundations.

IX    Panic is general. Heavy damage to masonry structures and to underground pipes. Large cracks open in ground.

X    Many buildings collapse. Water splashes over riverbanks.

XI–XII    Virtually total destruction.

1 No wine may be produced from a vine until its fourth year.
2 The vineyard, if within the biblical lands, must be left fallow every seven years.
3 Only grapes for wine may be grown in the vineyard.
4 From arrival at the winery, the grapes and resulting wine may only be handled by strictly Sabbath-observing Jews, and only 100 per cent kosher materials may be used in the wine making, maturation and bottling processes.

## APPELLATIONS FOR MARGARET THATCHER

Attila the Hen, Ayesha, Blessed Margaret, Boadicea, 'Er Indoors, Gladys Hacksaw, the Iron Lady, the Mekon, the Milk Snatcher, the Plutonium Blonde, Rhoda the Rhino, She Who Must Be Obeyed, Snobby Roberts, the Westminster Ripper. 'The eyes of Caligula...the mouth of Marilyn Monroe.' *Francois Mitterrand*

## THE SEVEN BRIDGES OF KONIGSBERG

In the lifetime of the remarkable Swiss mathematician Leonhard Euler (1707–1783), seven bridges crossed the Pregel River in Konigsberg, shown in the diagram below:

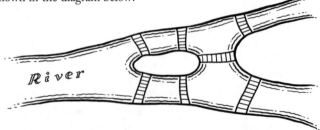

Euler asked whether or not it was possible to cross all seven bridges without passing twice on any bridge. Solution page 137.

*Primary qualities*: solidity, extension, figure, mobility, number.
*Secondary qualities*: colour, odour, sound, taste.

> *from 'An Essay Concerning Human Understanding'*
> *(1690) by John Locke*

## 221B BAKER STREET

Though there is no 221B Baker Street, the legendary address of Sir Arthur Conan Doyle's fictional detective Sherlock Holmes and his *amanuensis* Dr John Watson, Sherlockians take this to imply that the dwelling was disguised. The B is regarded as implying the French designation *bis*, meaning that the location was a subsidiary one, and the rooms as described in Watson's narratives were indeed upstairs. By steady accretions of detail from the stories, we know that they consisted of a sitting room, separate bedrooms and a projecting bow window overlooking Baker Street ('The Mazarin Stone'), and were equipped with gas ('The Copper Beeches'), a telephone ('The Three Garridebs') and an electric call-bell system ('The Mazarin Stone'). The sitting room featured a sideboard ('The Beryl Coronet'), bearskin hearthrug ('The Priory School'), wickerwork basketchair ('The Noble Client'). In the corner sat a deal-topped table on which reposed Holmes' bunsen-burner (*A Study in Scarlet*), gasogene ('A Scandal in Bohemia'), retort, pipette and litmus paper ('The Copper Beeches'). Holmes kept his cigars ('The Musgrave Ritual') and pipes ('The Mazarin Stone') in the coal-scuttle, his tobacco in the toe-end of a Persian slipper ('The Naval Treaty'); the mantelpiece in his bedroom was littered with syringes for cocaine ('The Dying Detective') and unanswered correspondence affixed with a large jack-knife ('The Musgrave Ritual'). Watson's decorations included pictures of General Gordon and the preacher Henry Ward Beecher ('The Cardboard Box'); Holmes, similarly patriotic, adorned the sitting-room wall with a 'VR' ('Victoria Regina') in bullet-pocks ('The Musgrave Ritual'). To their long-suffering Scottish landlady Mrs Hudson, the pair paid a 'princely' rent ('The Dying Detective').

Inspired by American science fiction writer Theodore Sturgeon (1918–1985). Asked why he wrote in his genre, 90 per cent of which was 'horseshit', he replied: 'Ninety per cent of everything is horseshit.'

## PHAR LAP

Chestnut gelding by Night Raid (sire) from Entreaty (dam), born 4 October 1926, Seadown Stud, Timaru, New Zealand ('Phar Lap' is a Thai expression meaning 'Lightning'). Sold in 1928 by A. F. Roberts to David Davis, who leased him for three years to trainer Harry Telford. Height: 17 hands. Weight of heart: 6.3 kg. Colours: red, black and white (1929–30); red and green (1931–32). Races: 53. First: 39. Second: 3. Third: 2. Unplaced: 9. First win at Rosehill 27 April 1929; from September 1929 was favourite in all but one race, winning fourteen races as a four-year-old. Jockey Jim Pike recorded twenty-seven wins in thirty rides. Won 1930 Melbourne Cup carrying 62.5 kg; finished eighth in 1931 Melbourne Cup carrying 68 kg, its last race in Australia. Died 5 April 1932 at Menlo Park, California. Official cause: colic. Winnings: £66,738. At the time the third greatest stake winner in the world after Sun Beau (USA) and Ksar (France).

## REFLECTIVENESS OF PAINT

| Colour | Light Reflected |
|---|---|
| White | 70–90% |
| Cream, ivory | 55–90% |
| Light yellow | 65–70% |
| Light green | 40–50% |
| Medium grey | 15–30% |
| Orange | 15–30% |
| Medium blue | 15–20% |
| Dark blue | 5–10% |
| Red | 3–18% |

*'It's strange how the most banal utterances sometimes make me marvel.'*
French novelist Gustave Flaubert (1821–1880) had an uncanny ear for
bourgeois cliche, which he brought to bear most memorably in his
*Dictionnaire des Idées reçues* (*The Dictionary of Received Ideas*). Intended
as a companion to his unfinished novel *Bouvard et Pécuchet,* Flaubert's
satirical lexicon of conversational prejudices was published post-
humously in 1911. Here is a selection:

| | |
|---|---|
| *absinthe* | Exceptionally violent poison: one glass and you're a dead man. Journalists drink it while writing their articles. Has killed more soldiers than the bedouins. |
| *beard* | A sign of strength. Too much beard causes baldness. Helps to protect ties. |
| *black* | Always followed by 'as ebony'. |
| *black women* | Hotter than white women. |
| *Crusades* | Benefited Venetian trade. |
| *English women* | Express surprise that they can have pretty children. |
| *French* | The greatest people in the world. |
| *illusions* | Pretend to have a great many, and complain that you have lost them all. |
| *Italians* | All musical. All treacherous. |
| *money* | Cause of all evil. *Uri sacra fames.* The god of the day—not to be confused with Apollo. Politicians call it emoluments; lawyers, retainers; doctors, fees; employees, salary; workmen, pay; servants, wages. 'Money is not happiness'. |
| *mushrooms* | Should be bought only at the market. |
| *old people* | When discussing a flood, thunderstorm, etc, they cannot remember ever having seen a worse one. |
| *sex* | Word to avoid. Say instead, 'Intimacy occurred...' |
| *stroll* | Always take one after dinner, it helps with digestion. |

Until 1910, Australian legal paper tender comprised notes issued by trading banks and one state government. The Australian Notes Act vested control of note issue in Commonwealth Treasury, then in 1924 in the board of the Commonwealth Bank. The Reserve Bank of Australia took responsibility when it was separated from the Commonwealth Bank in 1959; Note Printing Australia, an RBA subsidiary, was founded at Craigieburn, twenty-five kilometres north of Melbourne, in 1981. Paper's replacement by polymer substrate notes began in 1988, while the $1 and $2 notes were replaced by coins in 1984 and 1988 respectively. The current Australian note issue bears the images of the following:

$5 *Queen Elizabeth II*; Parliament House (aerial view).

$5 (Federation note) *Sir Henry Parkes* (1815–1896), convenor 1890 Federation conference; *Catherine Helen Spence* (1825–1910), journalist, social reformer, novelist.

$10 *A. B. 'Banjo' Paterson* (1864–1941), poet, journalist; *Dame Mary Gilmore* (1865–1962), poet.

$20 *Mary Reibey* (1777–1855), businesswoman, emancipist; *Reverend John Flynn* (1880–1951), founder of Royal Flying Doctor Service.

$50 *David Unaipon* (1872–1967), writer, inventor; *Edith Cowan* (1861–1932), first female member of an Australian parliament.

$100 *Dame Nellie Melba* (1861–1931), soprano; *Sir John Monash* (1865–1931), soldier, engineer, administrator.

## COMETS AND THEIR PERIOD OF ORBIT AROUND EARTH

Encke 3.3 years; Giacobini-Zinner 6.41 years; Grigg-Skjellerup 4.91 years; Halley 76.04 years; Pons-Winnecke 6.3 years; Schwassmann-Wachmann-1 16.10 years; Tempel-1 5.98 years; Tempel-2 5.26 years; Tempel-Tuttle 32.91 years; Whipple 7.46 years.

And here it is to be noted that men must be either pampered or crushed, because they can get revenge for small injuries but not grievous ones.

So a prudent man will always follow in the footsteps of great men and imitate those who have been outstanding. If his own prowess fails in comparison with theirs, at least it has an air of greatness about it.

So it should be noted that when he seizes a state the new ruler must determine all the injuries that he will need to inflict. He must inflict them once and for all, and not have to renew them every day, and in that way he will be able to set men's minds at rest and win them over to him when he confers benefits.

I shall only conclude that it is necessary for a prince to have the friendship of the people; otherwise he has no remedy in times of adversity.

It is better to be feared than loved.

He should appear to be compassionate, faithful to his word, kind, guileless and devout. And indeed he should be so. But his disposition should be such that, if he needs to be the opposite, he knows how.

*from* Il Principe (The Prince, *1513)*

NICKNAMES OF AFRICAN NATIONAL
FOOTBALL TEAMS

Algeria . . . . . . . . . . . . . . . . . . . . . *Les Fennecs* (The Desert Foxes)
Benin . . . . . . . . . . . . . . . . . . . . . . . . . . . . . *Ecureuils* (Squirrels)
Botswana. . . . . . . . . . . . . . . . . . . . . . . . . . . . . . . . . . . . . Zebras
Burkina Faso . . . . . . . . . . . . . . . . . . . . . *Les Etalons* (The Stallions)
Burundi. . . . . . . . . . . . . . . . . . . . . *Les Hirondelles* (The Sparrows)
Cameroon. . . . . . . . . . . . . *Lions Indomptables* (Indomitable Lions)
Congo . . . . . . . . . . . . . . . . . . . . . . . *Diables Rouges* (Red Devils)
Côte d'Ivoire . . . . . . . . . . . . . . . . . . . *Les Elephants* (The Elephants)

| | |
|---|---|
| Egypt | Pharaohs |
| Eritrea | Red Sea Boys |
| Ethiopia | Walyas |
| Gabon | *Les Panthères* (The Panthers) |
| Gambia | Scorpions |
| Ghana | Black Stars |
| Guinea | Syli Nationale Stars |
| Kenya | Harambee Stars |
| Lesotho | *Likuena* (Crocodiles) |
| Liberia | Lone Star |
| Libya | The Greens |
| Madagascar | Scorpions |
| Malawi | Flames |
| Mali | *Les Aigles* (The Eagles) |
| Mauritania | Mourabitounes |
| Mauritius | Club M |
| Morocco | *Lions de l'Atlas* (Atlas Lions) |
| Mozambique | *Mambas* (Snakes) |
| Namibia | Brave Warriors |
| Nigeria | Super Eagles |
| Rwanda | *Amavubi* (Wasps) |
| Senegal | Lions of Teranga |
| Sierra Leone | Leone Stars |
| Somalia | Ocean Stars |
| South Africa | *Bafana Bafana* (The Boys) |
| Sudan | *Sokoor Al-Jediane* (Falcons of Jediane) |
| Swaziland | Sihlangu Semnikati Sitsebe |
| Tanzania | Taifa Stars |
| Togo | *Les Eperviers* (Hawks) |
| Tunisia | *Les Aigles de Carthage* (Carthage Eagles) |
| Uganda | Cranes |
| Zambia | *Chipolopolo* (Bullets) |
| Zimbabwe | Warriors |

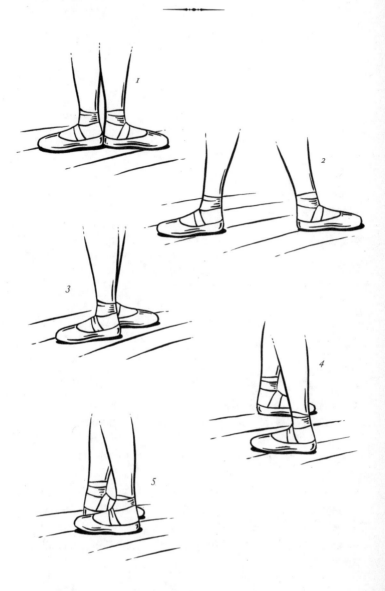

*Active Penguins Seek The Nearest Deep Pool*
OSI model (computer science): Application—Presentation—Session—Transport—Network—Data Link—Physical.

ARROWE
Documentation required on aircraft: Air worthiness certificate—Radio licence—Registration—Owner's Manual—Weight and balance—Equipment list.

CAMEL
Five measures of a bank's viability: Capital adequacy—Asset quality—Management quality—Earnings—Liquidity.

COP IS ME
Circumstances in which a search warrant is unnecessary: Consent—Open view—Public place—Incidental to lawful arrest—Suspicious person—Mobile premises—Emergency.

*Eat An Aspirin After A Night-time Snack*
The Seven Continents: Europe—Antarctica—Asia—Africa—Australia—North America—South America.

*Empty Garbage Before Dad Flips; Every Good Boy Deserves Favour*
Notes represented by the lines on the treble staff, from bottom.

*King Philip Came Over For Good Sex; Kingfish, Pickerel, Catfish Over Flowed God's Seas; Kings Play Cards On Fat Girls Stomachs; Keep People Coming On For Good-Sized Violins*
A guide to the biological groups in taxonomy: Kingdom—Phylum—Class—Order—Family—Genus—Species (and Variety).

*Lazy French Tarts Lie Naked In Anticipation Of Sex*
Structures passing through the skull's superior orbital fissure: Lacrimal nerve—Frontal nerve—Trochlear nerve—Lateral nerve—Nasociliary nerve—Internal nerve—Abducens nerve—Ophthalmic veins—Sympathetic nerves.

*Oh My, Such Good Apple Pie, Sweet As Sugar*
Dicarboxylic acids: Oxalic—Malonic—Succinic—Glutaric—Adipic—Pimelic—Suberic—Azelaic—Sebacic.

*Lucky Cows Drink Milk*
Roman numbers, in ascending order: L (50)—C (100)—D (500)—M (1000).

*Please Excuse My Dear Aunt Sally*
Order of operations in mathematics: Parentheses—Exponents—Multiplication—Division—Addition—Subtraction.

ROY G. BIV; *Richard Of York Gave Battle In Vain*
Colours of the spectrum: Red—Orange—Yellow—Green—Blue—Indigo—Violet.

*Some Lovers Try Positions That They Can't Handle*
Order of the bones in the wrist: Scaphoid—Lunate—Triquetral—Pisiform—Trapezium—Trapezoid—Capitate—Hamate.

*Toronto Girls Can Flirt And Other Queer Things Can Do*
Mohs hardness scale: Talc—Gypsum—Calcite—Fluorite—Apatite—Orthoclase Feldspar—Quartz—Topaz—Corundum—Diamond.

*True Virgins Make Dull Company*
Computing course: True heading minus Variation plus or minus Magnetic variation plus or minus Deviation equals Course.

*Two Zulus Bruised My Cervix; To Zanzibar By Motor Car*
Branches of the facial nerve: Temporal—Zygomatic—Buccal—Mandibular—Cervical.

## THE FUJITA SCALE

The Fujita scale was devised by Tetsuya Theodore Fujita (1920–1998), a Japanese meteorologist recruited to the University of Chicago in the early 1950s and subsequently credited with revolutionising American climatology. The Fujita scale was devised in the 1970s to help the National Weather Service measure tornado intensities; before this all tornadoes were counted as equals.

| F-scale Number | Intensity Phrase | Wind Speed | Damage |
|---|---|---|---|
| F0 | Gale tornado | 40–72 mph (65–113 kmh) | Some damage to chimneys; breaks branches off trees, pushes over shallow-rooted trees; damages sign boards. |
| F1 | Moderate tornado | 73–112 mph (117–180 kmh) | The lower limit is the beginning of hurricane wind-speed; peels surface off roofs; mobile homes pushed off foundations or overturned; moving autos pushed off the roads; attached garages may be destroyed. |
| F2 | Significant tornado | 113–157 mph (182–253 kmh) | Considerable damage. Roofs torn off frame houses; mobile homes demolished; boxcars pushed over; large trees snapped or uprooted; light object missiles generated. |
| F3 | Severe tornado | 158–206 mph (254–330 kmh) | Roof and some walls torn off well constructed houses; trains overturned; most trees in forest uprooted. |
| F4 | Devastating tornado | 207–260 mph (333–418 kmh) | Well-constructed houses levelled; structures with weak foundations blown off some distance; cars thrown and large missiles generated. |
| F5 | Incredible tornado | 261–318 mph (420–512 kmh) | Strong frame houses lifted off foundations and carried considerable distances to disintegrate; automobile-sized missiles fly through the air in excess of 100 metres; trees debarked; steel reinforced concrete structures badly damaged. |
| F6 | Inconceivable tornado | 319–379 mph (513–610 kmh) | These winds are very unlikely. If this level is ever achieved, evidence for it might only be found in some manner of ground swirl pattern, for it may never be identifiable through engineering studies. |

| *Beatified Name* | *Original Name* |
| --- | --- |
| Saint Ambrose | Ambrosius[1] |
| Saint Augustine | Aurelius Augustinus[1] |
| Saint Bernadette | Marie Bernarde Soubirous[2] |
| Saint Bonaventure | Giovanni di Fidanza[1] |
| Saint Catherine of Siena | Caterina Benincasa[3] |
| Saint Columba | Colmcille[4] |
| Saint Francis of Assisi | Giovanni Francesco Bernardone[5] |
| Saint Jerome | Eusebius Hieronymous[1] |
| Saint John of the Cross | Juan de Yepes y Alvarez[3] |
| Saint Macarius of Petra | Arius[1] |
| Saint Mary Magdalen | Catherine Mary Magdalen dei Pazzi[3] |
| Saint Matthew | Levi[6] |
| Saint Nicholas | Nicholas of Bari[1] |
| Saint Peter | Simon[6] |
| Saint Perpetua | Vibia Perpetua[7] |
| Saint Severinus | Anicius Mnalius Severinus Boethius[7] |
| Saint Teresa of Avila | Teresa de Cepeda y Ahumada[3] |
| Saint Theresa of Lisieux | Thérèse Martin[8] |
| Saint Thomas of Hereford | Thomas Cantilupe[1] |
| Saint, The | Simon Templar[9] |
| Yves Saint-Laurent | Henri Donat Mathieu[10] |

1 Doctor/bishop; 2 First witness to Our Lady of Lourdes; 3 Mystic; 4 Missionary; 5 Stigmatic; 6 Apostle; 7 Martyr; 8 Carmelite nun proclaimed 'the greatest saint of modern times' by Pope Pius XI; 9 Fictional secret agent, creation of Leslie Charteris (1907–1993); 10 Acclaimed French fashion designer, born 1936, originally a protege of Christian Dior.

Birth weight: 2.26 kg[1]

Population of Tupelo at the time of his birth: 6000

Elvis's lucky number: 8

Columbia's unsuccessful bid for Elvis in 1955: $15,000

Number of teddy bears he received for Christmas in 1956: 282

Elvis's army serial number: 53310761[2]

Size of Elvis's combat boots: 12

Number of layers in his 1.52m tall wedding cake when he married Priscilla Beaulieu in Milton Prell's suite at Las Vegas's Aladdin Hotel on 1 May 1967: 6

Value of jewellery distributed by Elvis during his performances at Asheville, North Carolina (22–24 July 1975): $US220,000

Elvis's peak tax bracket: 91 per cent

Elvis's phone numbers (given to US president Richard Nixon on 21 December 1970 when the singer sought a Narcotics Bureau badge): 278-3496, 278-5935 (Beverly Hills); 397-4427, 398-4882, 398-9722 (Memphis); 325-3241 (Palm Springs)

Number of narcotic and amphetamine pills Dr George Nichopolous prescribed to Elvis from 20 January to 16 August 1977: 5684

Number of portraits of Elvis at Graceland at the time of his death: 17

Number plate of Elvis's gold Cadillac: 2X-139

Registration number of his Convair 880: N880EP

Number plate of Elvis's hearse: 1-C5652

Cars in funeral procession: 49 including sixteen limousines[3]

Cost of Elvis's funeral: $23,789.73

---

1 Same as Hank Williams; 2 Subject of the song 'Dear 53310761' by the Threeteens (Rev 3516) in 1958; 3 Sixteen also the number of coaches in the Herman Parker/Sam Phillips song 'Mystery Train', which Elvis recorded on 11 July 1955.

———•◦•———

Having cancelled the 1973 New Year's honours list upon winning
office, the Whitlam government created a three-tier 'Order of
Australia' along lines of a similar honour system in Canada: Her
Majesty the Queen was Sovereign of the Order, Governor-General Sir
John Kerr the Chancellor and Principal Companion. The first investi-
ture, however, was delayed by Kerr's dismissal of the government, and
further changes were announced by the succeeding administration of
Malcolm Fraser: the titles Knight (AK) and Dame (AD) were introduced as the senior honour, the Australian Medal (OAM) added as the
most junior. Imperial honours were also resumed, only to cease again
after Bob Hawke became prime minister in March 1983; he also elim-
inated the titles of Knight and Dame. The fourteen holding the
discontinued designations AK or AD, with their dates of award, are as
follows:

Barwick, Garfield (Edward John) AK. . . . . . . . . . . . . . 8 June 1981

Burnet, (Frank) MacFarlane AK . . . . . . . . . . . . . . 26 January 1978

Court, Charles (Walter Michael) AK . . . . . . . . . . . . . 14 June 1982

Cowen, Zelman AK . . . . . . . . . . . . . . . . . . . . . . 8 December 1977

Cutler, (Arthur) Roden AK. . . . . . . . . . . . . . . . . . . . 7 April 1981

Hasluck, Alexandra (Margaret Martin) AD . . . . . . . . . 6 June 1978

Jackson, Gordon AK . . . . . . . . . . . . . . . . . . . . . . . . 13 June 1983

Kerr, John (Robert) AK . . . . . . . . . . . . . . . . . . . . . . 24 May 1976

Lyons, Enid (Muriel) AD . . . . . . . . . . . . . . . . . . . 26 January 1980

Menzies, Robert (Gordon) AK. . . . . . . . . . . . . . . . . . 7 June 1976

HRH Prince of Wales, Charles AK. . . . . . . . . . . . . 14 March 1981

Stephen, Ninian (Martin) AK. . . . . . . . . . . . . . . . . . 29 July 1982

Syme, Colin (York) AK . . . . . . . . . . . . . . . . . . . . . . . 6 June 1977

Wright, (Roy) Douglas AK . . . . . . . . . . . . . . . . . 26 January 1983

Phrenology is the belief that personality and intellect consist of a number of independent, inborn mental 'faculties', each localising in a different part of the brain. It was first advanced in 1796 by the Austrian anatomist Franz Joseph Gall (1758–1828); his lectures became so popular that they were banned by government order. Gall

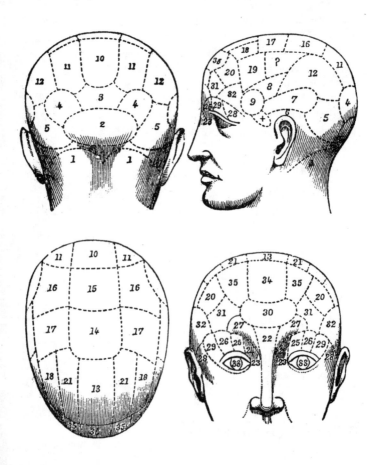

and his acolytes, chiefly the German physician Johann Gaspar Spurzheim (1776–1832), believed that an examination of skull bumps would reveal a person's character, and to a degree their destiny. Among believers were naturalist Alfred Russel Wallace (1823–1913), co-proposer of the theory of natural selection, and poet Walt Whitman (1819–1892), who filled his *Leaves of Grass* with phrenological terms ('O adhesiveness—O pulse of my life'). As a child Australian prime minister Sir Robert Menzies had his skull 'read' and the phrenologist purportedly foresaw skills as an orator. *Phrenology: Fad and Science*, by John Davies (1955) is a lively history, recording the growth in its belief and its steady debunking.

AFFECTIVE

I. *Propensities*

1. Amativeness (sexual love); 2. Philoprogenitiveness (love of offspring); 3. Inhabitiveness (love of native place); 4. Adhesiveness (attachment and gregariousness); 5. Combativeness (aggression); 6. Destructiveness; 7. Secretiveness; 8. Acquisitiveness; 9. Constructiveness.

II. *Sentiments*

10. Self-esteem; 11. Love of approbation (desire for good opinion); 12. Cautiousness; 13. Benevolence; 14. Veneration (tendency to consider others greater than oneself); 15. Firmness (fortitude and perseverance); 16. Conscientiousness (incitement to justice); 17. Hope (gaiety and cheerfulness); 18. Wonder (propensity to dream); 19. Ideality (delight in the perfect and exquisite); 20. Wit (also known as Sentiment of the Ludicrous); 21. Imitation (propensity to mimic).

INTELLECTUAL

I. *Perceptive*

22. Individuality (ability to distinguish objects); 23. Form (ability to recognise faces and figures); 24. Size; 25. Weight; 26. Colour; 27. Locality; 28. Number; 29. Order; 30. Eventuality; 31. Time; 32. Tune; 33. Language.

II. *Reflective*

34. Comparison; 35. Causality.

——•◦•——

Cash in—Check out—Croak—Cross over—Cut One's Stick—Drop the Hooks—Go Home in a Box—Go the Way of All Flesh—Go up Salt River—Go West—Hop the Last Rattler—Kick the Bucket—Pass out of the Picture—Pay the Debt of Nature—Push Up Daisies—Rest in Abraham's Bosom—Ride the Pale Horse—Take the Big Jump—Toss in One's Alley


## GOLDWYNISMS

——•◦•——

*Polish-born Samuel Goldwyn (1882–1974), originally Samuel Goldfisch, was founder of one of the constituents of what became Metro-Goldwyn-Mayer, and a solo producer of about seventy films over thirty-five years, including* Wuthering Heights *(1938),* The Secret Life of Walter Mitty *(1946) and* Guys and Dolls *(1955). Yet perhaps his most enduring legacy is a string of malapropisms which may or may not be apocryphal.*

Include me out.

*I can tell you in two words: Im Possible.*

A verbal agreement isn't worth the paper it's written on.

*I never put on a pair of shoes until I've worn them at least five years.*

A man who goes to a psychiatrist should have his head examined.

*They're always biting the hand that lays the golden egg.*

I don't think anybody should write his autobiography until after he's dead.

*She's colossal in a small way.*

Our comedies are not to be laughed at.

*The trouble with this business is the dearth of bad pictures.*

I read part of it all the way through.

*This atom bomb is dynamite.*

Every Tom, Dick and Harry is named Sam.

*Talipes varus*. . . . . . . . . . . . . . . . . . . . . . . . . . . . foot turning inward
*Talipes valgus*. . . . . . . . . . . . . . . . . . . . . . . . . . . foot turning outward
*Talipes equinus*. . . . . . foot turning downwards with elevation of heel
*Talipes calcaneus*. . . . . . foot turning upwards with depression of heel

## TEN PEOPLE BEST KNOWN FOR A COMMON EXPRESSION

Robert Anderson (1917– ): 'Tea and sympathy.' Title of play, 1957.

Stella Benson (1892–1933), novelist: 'Call no man foe but never love a stranger.' From *This Is the End*, 1917.

E. Y. Harburg (1898–1981), songwriter: 'Brother, can you spare a dime?' Title of song, 1932.

L. P. Hartley (1895–1972), novelist: 'The past is a foreign country: they do things differently there.' Opening lines to *The Go-Between*, 1953.

John Gillespie Magee (1922–1941), American airman: 'Oh! I have slipped the surly bonds of earth.' In his poem 'High Flight'.

George Leigh Mallory (1886–1924), mountaineer: 'Because it's there.' Asked why he wished to climb Everest, 1923.

Mrs Manley (1663–1724), dramatist: 'No time like the present.' In *The Lost Lover*, 1696.

Thomas Middleton (c. 1580–1627), dramatist: 'Anything for a Quiet Life.' Title of play, c. 1620.

Richard Rowland (c. 1881–1947), film producer: 'The lunatics have taken over the asylum.' After Charles Chaplin, Mary Pickford, Douglas Fairbanks Snr and others established United Artists in 1919.

George Villiers (1628–1687), dramatist: 'Ay, now the plot thickens very much upon us.' *The Rehearsal*, 1671.

## FIVE FORCES

*In* The Competitive Advantage of Nations *(1990), Harvard management theorist Michael Porter outlines the following as the five key forces that drive competition:*

1  Existing rivalry between firms.
2  Threat of new entrants to market.
3  Threat of substitute products and services.
4  Bargaining power of suppliers.
5  Bargaining power of buyers.

## GUITARISTS

In *Mojo* music magazine's June 1996 issue, a group of expert contributors selected the 100 greatest rock guitarists of all time. The best ten, and their guitars, were as follows:

1. Jimi Hendrix ....................... Fender Stratocaster
2. Steve Cropper ......................... Fender Telecaster
3. Peter Green........................... Gibson Les Paul
4. Keith Richards........................ Fender Telecaster
5. Chuck Berry........................... Gibson ES-350
6. Eric Clapton ......................... Fender Stratocaster
7. Jimmy Page........................... Gibson Les Paul
8. T-Bone Walker......................... Gibson ES-150
9. Neil Young ........................... Gibson Les Paul
10. Richard Thompson ................... Fender Stratocaster

## THE GIANT RAT OF SUMATRA

A story for which the world is not yet prepared.

*Apollo Bay* (Victorian coastal town): schooner captained by the bay's discoverer Captain Loutit in 1845.

*Austins Ferry* (Hobart suburb): named for James Austin's ferry service, which commenced in 1818.

*Eden Hills* (Adelaide suburb): barque *Eden*, whose captain was granted land in the area in 1839.

*Esperance* (WA town): Huon de Kermadec's barque *L'Esperance*.

*Glenhuntly* (Melbourne suburb): barque which arrived in Hobson's Bay in 1839 with its passengers gripped by typhus.

*Larpent* (Victorian rural township): immigrant ship that landed 210 settlers at Geelong in 1849.

*Lucinda* (Queensland resort town): named for government steam yacht in the early twentieth century.

*Mount Nelson* (Hobart suburb): brig *Lady Nelson* which brought the first settlers to the area.

*Port Fairy* (Victorian coastal town): cutter *Fairy* which sheltered in its port in 1826.

*Port Victoria* (SA coastal town): schooner *Victoria* used by Adelaide Survey Association.

*Rosebud* (Melbourne suburb): schooner wrecked on offshore sandbank in 1851.

*St Kilda* (Melbourne suburb): reputedly after schooner *Our Lady of St Kilda*, familiar in Port Phillip Bay when area first surveyed in 1842.

*Scarborough* (Perth suburb): reputedly after transport ship of First Fleet in 1788.

*Success* (Perth suburb): vessel in which Captain James Stirling first visited Swan River in 1827.

*Victor Harbor* (SA town): vessel in which Captain Richard Crozier charted the harbour in 1837.

| Number | From Greek | From Latin |
|---|---|---|
| $^1/_2$ | hemi- | semi- |
| 1 | mono- | uni- |
| $1^1/_2$ | | sesqui- |
| 2 | di- | bi- |
| 3 | | ter-, tri- |
| 4 | tetra- | quadri- |
| 5 | penta- | quinque- |
| 6 | hexa- | sex- |
| 7 | hepta- | septi- |
| 8 | octo- | octa- |
| 9 | | nona- |
| 10 | deca-, deka- | |
| many | poly- | multi- |
| all | | omni- |

## PERSONALITIES OF SYBIL

Perhaps history's most famous psychiatric patient, Sybil Isabel Dorsett revealed to her therapist Dr Cornelia Wilbur another fifteen personalities in the course of an eleven-year analysis. These personalities, which became the *dramatis personae* of F. R. Schreiber's book *Sybil* in 1973 (and an Emmy Award-winning telemovie three years later, starring Joanne Woodward and Sally Field) were: Victoria Antoinette Scharleau; Peggy Lou Baldwin; Peggy Ann Baldwin; Mary Lucinda Saunders Dorsett; Marcia Lynn Dorsett; Vanessa Gail Dorsett; Mike Dorsett; Sid Dorsett; Nancy Lou Ann Baldwin; Sybil Ann Dorsett; Ruthie Dorsett; Clara Dorsett; Helen Dorsett; Marjorie Dorsett; The Blond.

It was revealed in March 1998 that the original of Dorsett had been Shirley Mason (1923–1998) of Lexington, Kentucky. A friend of Schreiber's, she had gone on to a successful career as an art teacher and painter.

Burhan Belge (1937–41); Conrad Hilton (1942–47)[1]; George Sanders (1949–54)[2]; Herbert Hutner (1962–66); Joshua S. Cosden, Jr (1966–67); Jack Ryan (1975–76); Michael O'Hara (1976–82); Felipe De Alba (1982)[3]; Prince Frederick von Anhalt (1986–2002).

---

1 One daughter; 2 Sanders later married Gabor's sister Magda; 3 Not legal: she was still married.

Asked how many husbands she'd had, Gabor is alleged to have replied: 'Apart from my own?'


## HINTS TO FOOTBALLERS

*Two years after Thomas Wills' famous letter of exhortation in* Bell's Life in Victoria, *the following was printed as advice to players of the new code of Victorian Rules football in the* Victorian Cricketers' Guide *of 1860:*

If an adversary is running with the ball, kick him over unceremoniously if you can't knock it out of his hand.

In making a kick from your hand, let your toe catch the ball the instant it leaves the ground. With a little practice this will be found easy, elegant and effectual.

Practice kicking with both feet. Many goals are lost through being able to use only one, and the left foot will be found particularly convenient when the ball has lee-way on it.

Never allow boys to play amongst men. They spoil the game, no one likes to rush them and yet they are almost certain to get hurt.

If the ball be near your own goal, kick it as much on one side as possible but not behind you if you can help it as this is considered cowardly play.

———•••———

Cross and Crown—Puss-In-The-Corner—Goose Tracks—Bourgoyne Surrounded—Hen and Chickens—Pine Tree—Bear's Tracks—Flying Dutchman—Peony—Feather Star—Flying Geese—Drunkard's Path—Lincoln's Platform—Robbing Peter to Pay Paul—Stepping Stones—Dutchman's Puzzle—Morning Star—Wheel of Fortune—King David's Crown—Cats and Mice—Joseph's Coat—Hearts and Gizzards—Jacob's Ladder—Grandmother's Fan—Dresden Plate—Delectable Mountains—Winding Warp—Log Cabin—Turkey's Tracks—Rose of Sharon—Irish Chain

## DEATHS IN LONDON 12–19 SEPTEMBER 1665

———•••———

*Four hundred years ago, the city of London began collecting what it called 'Bills of Mortality': a weekly compilation of births and deaths which became the first serious attempt at statistical sampling, and the subject of the first significant work of statistics, John Graunt's* Natural and Political Observations Made upon the Bills of Mortality. *This is a tabulation of the causes of death in London during a week at the height of the Black Plague:*

| | |
|---|---:|
| Abortive | 1 |
| Aged | 43 |
| Ague | 2 |
| Apoplexie | 1 |
| Bleeding | 2 |
| Burnt in His Bed by a Candle at St Giles Cripplegate | 1 |
| Canker | 2 |
| Childbed | 42 |
| Chrisomes | 18 |
| Consumption | 134 |
| Convulsion | 64 |
| Cough | 2 |

Dropsie . . . . . . . . . . . . . . . . . . . . . . . . . . . . . . . . . . . . . . . . . . . . . 33
Feaver. . . . . . . . . . . . . . . . . . . . . . . . . . . . . . . . . . . . . . . . . . . . . . . 309
Flox and Small-pox . . . . . . . . . . . . . . . . . . . . . . . . . . . . . . . . . . . 5
Frighted . . . . . . . . . . . . . . . . . . . . . . . . . . . . . . . . . . . . . . . . . . . . . . 3
Gowt . . . . . . . . . . . . . . . . . . . . . . . . . . . . . . . . . . . . . . . . . . . . . . . . . 1
Grief . . . . . . . . . . . . . . . . . . . . . . . . . . . . . . . . . . . . . . . . . . . . . . . . . 3
Griping in the Guts . . . . . . . . . . . . . . . . . . . . . . . . . . . . . . . . . . 51
Iaundies . . . . . . . . . . . . . . . . . . . . . . . . . . . . . . . . . . . . . . . . . . . . . . 5
Imposthume. . . . . . . . . . . . . . . . . . . . . . . . . . . . . . . . . . . . . . . . . 11
Infants . . . . . . . . . . . . . . . . . . . . . . . . . . . . . . . . . . . . . . . . . . . . . . 16
Killed by Fall from Bellfry at Allhallowes the Great . . . . . . . . . . . 1
Kingsevil . . . . . . . . . . . . . . . . . . . . . . . . . . . . . . . . . . . . . . . . . . . . 2
Lethargy . . . . . . . . . . . . . . . . . . . . . . . . . . . . . . . . . . . . . . . . . . . . 1
Palsie . . . . . . . . . . . . . . . . . . . . . . . . . . . . . . . . . . . . . . . . . . . . . . . 1
Plague . . . . . . . . . . . . . . . . . . . . . . . . . . . . . . . . . . . . . . . . . . . . 716
Rickets. . . . . . . . . . . . . . . . . . . . . . . . . . . . . . . . . . . . . . . . . . . . . 17
Rising of the Lights . . . . . . . . . . . . . . . . . . . . . . . . . . . . . . . . . 11
Scowring . . . . . . . . . . . . . . . . . . . . . . . . . . . . . . . . . . . . . . . . . . . 5
Scurvy . . . . . . . . . . . . . . . . . . . . . . . . . . . . . . . . . . . . . . . . . . . . . . 2
Spleen . . . . . . . . . . . . . . . . . . . . . . . . . . . . . . . . . . . . . . . . . . . . . . 1
Spotted Feaver . . . . . . . . . . . . . . . . . . . . . . . . . . . . . . . . . . . . . 101
Stilborn . . . . . . . . . . . . . . . . . . . . . . . . . . . . . . . . . . . . . . . . . . . . 17
Stone . . . . . . . . . . . . . . . . . . . . . . . . . . . . . . . . . . . . . . . . . . . . . . . 2
Stopping of the Stomach . . . . . . . . . . . . . . . . . . . . . . . . . . . . . 9
Strangury. . . . . . . . . . . . . . . . . . . . . . . . . . . . . . . . . . . . . . . . . . . 1
Suddenly . . . . . . . . . . . . . . . . . . . . . . . . . . . . . . . . . . . . . . . . . . . 1
Surfeit . . . . . . . . . . . . . . . . . . . . . . . . . . . . . . . . . . . . . . . . . . . . . 49
Teeth . . . . . . . . . . . . . . . . . . . . . . . . . . . . . . . . . . . . . . . . . . . . . 121
Thresh . . . . . . . . . . . . . . . . . . . . . . . . . . . . . . . . . . . . . . . . . . . . . . 5
Timpany . . . . . . . . . . . . . . . . . . . . . . . . . . . . . . . . . . . . . . . . . . . . 2
Tiffick . . . . . . . . . . . . . . . . . . . . . . . . . . . . . . . . . . . . . . . . . . . . . 12
Vomiting . . . . . . . . . . . . . . . . . . . . . . . . . . . . . . . . . . . . . . . . . . . 3
Winde . . . . . . . . . . . . . . . . . . . . . . . . . . . . . . . . . . . . . . . . . . . . . . 3
Wormes . . . . . . . . . . . . . . . . . . . . . . . . . . . . . . . . . . . . . . . . . . . 15

'I said I was the greatest, not the smartest.' Thus Muhammad Ali (aka Cassius Clay) after failing the US Army's intelligence test. Yet Ali's ringcraft was often matched by his rhyme-craft; here is a selection of his odes:

This is the legend of Cassius Clay
The most beautiful fighter in the world today.
He talks a great deal and he brags indeed
Of a muscular punch that's incredible in speed.
This brash young boxer is something to see
And the heavyweight championship is his destiny
He is the greatest!

*before fighting Sonny Liston, February 1964*

From all over the world they send their best
To battle Ali for the ultimate Test.
Now merry olde England is sending her hero
Big Joe Bugner, whose chances are zero.
Now Big Joe, he can swing, he can roll
But with Muhammad Ali in there, the ring is too small.
Since when could a bug handle a bee
A bee that's pretty and quick as me.
Bugs fly through the air with the greatest of ease
But this is one bug who will be on his knees…

*February 1973*

This might shock and amaze ya
But I'm going to re-tire Joe Frazier

*January 1974*

I like your show and I like your style
But your pay's so bad I won't be back for a while

*to Michael Parkinson, March 1971*

*Names commonly given to residents of a place*

| Demonym | Place |
| --- | --- |
| *Apple Islanders* | Tasmania, Australia |
| *Aquisextain* | Aix-en-Provence, France |
| *Aturin* | Aire-sur-l'Adour, France |
| *Banana Bender* | Queensland, Australia |
| *Bellifontain* | Fontainebleu, France |
| *Burkinabé* | Burkina Faso |
| *Cairene* | Cairo, Egypt |
| *Cestrian* | Chester, England |
| *Cisestrian* | Chichester, England |
| *Cabbage Patcher* | Victoria, Australia |
| *Cornstalk* | New South Wales, Australia |
| *Crow-Eater* | South Australia, Australia |
| *Delhite* | New Delhi, India |
| *Dorpia* | Schenectady, New York, USA |
| *Edinburgher* | Edinburgh, Scotland |
| *Emirian* | Dubai, United Arab Emirates |
| *Gallovidian* | Galway, Ireland |
| *Geordie* | Newcastle-upon-Tyne, England |
| *Hoosier* | Indiana, USA |
| *Lexoviens* | Lisieux, France |
| *Mancunian* | Manchester, England |
| *Monegsque* | Monte Carlo, Monaco |
| *Moonraker* | Wiltshire, England |
| *Moose Javian* | Moose Jaw, USA |
| *Novocastrian* | Newcastle, Australia |
| *Okie* | Oklahoma, USA |
| *Salopian* | Shropshire, England |
| *Sandgroper* | Western Australia, Australia |
| *Scouse* | Liverpool, England |
| *Top-Ender* | Northern Territory, Australia |
| *Zonian* | American in Panama |

1 Mariana Trench, Pacific Ocean, 35,827 ft (10,920m)
2 Puerto Rico Trench, Atlantic Ocean, 30,246 ft (9218m)
3 Java Trench, Indian Ocean, 24,460 ft (7455m)
4 Arctic Basin, Arctic Ocean, 18,456 ft (5625m)

## UNUSUAL CHESS OPENINGS

Meadow Hay Opening 1. a4
Orang-Utan Opening 1. b4
The Fred 1. e4 f5 2. exf5 Kf7
The Gotcha 1. d4 c5 2. d5 Nf6 3. Nf3 c4
The Spike 1. g4
The Woozle 1. d4 c5 2. d5 Nf6 3. Nc3 Qa5
Bird's Bastard 1. f4

## SUPERHEROES

The inaugural popular superhero was the Gladiator, conceived by Philip Gordon Wylie (1902–1971), the son of a Presbyterian minister, in 1930. It revived the mythological idea of a young man with abnormal powers and strength—in this case a puny college boy who obtained such gifts from consuming a chemical serum. When *The Gladiator* was made into a film of the same name eight years later, it sparked the first of a host of comic-book imitators. The dozen most significant are: *Superman* (1938), *Human Torch* (1939), *Batman* (1939), *Captain Marvel* (1940), *Captain America* (1941), *Wonder Woman* (1942), *Plastic Man* (1944), *The Fantastic Four* (1961), *The Incredible Hulk* (1962), *The Amazing Spider-Man* (1963), *The Silver Surfer* (1968), *The Flash* (1990).

*Geologists divide the Earth's 4.5-billion-year history into pre-Cambrian and Phaneozoic time, and then into Eras, Periods and Epochs—in that order.*

| Name | Millions of Years Ago |
|---|---|
| Hadean Era | 4500–3800 |
| Archaean Era | 3800–2500 |
| Proterozoic Era | 2500–543 |
| Paleozoic Era | 543–248 |
|     Cambrian Period | 543–490 |
|     Ordovician Period | 490–443 |
|     Silurian Period | 443–417 |
|     Devonian Period | 417–354 |
|     Carboniferous Period | 354–290 |
|     Permian Period | 290–248 |
| Mesozoic Era | 248–65 |
|     Triassic Period | 248–206 |
|     Jurassic Period | 206–144 |
|     Cretaceous Period | 144–65 |
| Cenozoic Era | 65–present |
|     Tertiary Period | 65–1.8 |
|     Quaternary Period | 1.8 million years ago–present |

## BED NAMES AND SIZES

Compact single  75 × 190cm

Popular single  90 × 190cm

Compact double  120 × 190cm

Popular double  135 × 190cm

Queen Size  150 × 200cm

King Size  180 × 200cm

Pitch—Duration—Intensity—Timbre

ISMS

| | |
|---|---|
| *Adiaphorism* | Tolerance of an action the Bible does not strictly prohibit. |
| *Bruxism* | Teeth grinding during sleep. |
| *Dispensationalism* | Belief in history as a sequence of divine arrangements. |
| *Eremetism* | Practice of living in seclusion. |
| *Fortuitism* | The belief that natural adaptations occur by chance, not design. |
| *Joe Millerism* | The practice of making bad or stale jokes. |
| *Lipogrammatism* | The practice of creating lipograms: writings that omit all words with a certain letter of the alphabet. |
| *Mecism* | Abnormal prolongation of a part of the body. |
| *Mugwumpism* | Acting as a political independent rather than a party member. |
| *Nice-Nellyism* | Prudishness. |
| *Oslerism* | The theory that a man is useless after the age of sixty. |
| *Pantagruelism* | Pejorative term for medicine. |
| *Patripassianism* | Christian doctrine that God shared the sufferings of Christ. |
| *Polymastism* | The presence of more than two breasts. |
| *Psittacism* | Repetitive, mechanical, meaningless speech. |
| *Rhotacism* | Faulty pronunciation of the letter 'r'. |
| *Slurvianism* | Slurred speech. |
| *Theanthropism* | The act of being both God and man. |
| *Xerophytism* | Characteristics of a plant that can grow in dry conditions. |

A scale for assessing asteroid and comet collision hazard agreed at a June 1999 international conference concerning near-Earth objects held in Torino (Turin), Italy. The brainchild of Professor Richard P. Binzel, from the Massachusetts Institute of Technology (MIT), it is divided into eleven risk intensities in White, Green, Yellow, Orange and Red bands.

*White: Events having no likely consequences*

0. Likelihood of collision is zero or well below the chance that random object of the same size will strike the Earth in the next few decades.

*Green: Events meriting careful monitoring*

1. Chance of a collision extremely unlikely, about the same as the chance of a random object of the same size striking the Earth in the next few decades.

*Yellow: Events meriting concern*

2. Somewhat close but not unusual encounter. Collision very unlikely.
3. A close encounter with 1 per cent or greater chance of collision causing localised destruction.
4. A close encounter with 1 per cent or greater chance of collision causing regional devastation.

*Orange: Threatening events*

5. A close encounter with a significant threat of collision causing regional devastation.
6. A close encounter with a significant threat of collision causing a global catastrophe.
7. A close encounter with an extremely significant threat of collision capable of causing a global catastrophe.

*Red: Certain collisions*

8. A collision capable of causing localised destruction. Such events occur on Earth between once per fifty years and once per 1000 years.
9. A collision capable of causing regional devastation. Such events occur on Earth between once per 1000 years and once per 100,000 years.
10. A collision capable of causing a global climatic catastrophe. Such events occur on Earth every 100,000 years or less often.

To atone for killing his children in a rage, Hercules was instructed by the Delphic oracle to serve Eurystheus, King of the Tiryns, for twelve years. For Eurystheus, he undertook the following labours.

*The Nemean Lion* . . . . . . . . . . . . . . . . . . . . . . . . . . . . . . strangled.

*The Lernean Hydra* . . . . . . . progressively decipitated and cauterised.

*The Arcadian Stag* . . . . . . . . . . . . . . . . . . . . . . . . . captured alive.

*The Erymanthian Boar* . . . driven into snowdrift and caught in a net.

*The Augean Stables* . . . . . . . . . . . . . . . . . cleaned by diverted river.

*The Styphalian Birds* . . . . . . . . . . frightened into air with rattle then shot with arrows.

*The Cretan Bull* . . . . . . . . . . . . . . roped and taken back to Greece.

*The Mares of Diomedes* . . . . . . . . . . Tamed when fed on the flesh of their owner, King Diomedes.

*The Girdle of Hippolyta* . . . . . . . girdle won in fight with Hippolyta, queen of the Amazons.

*The Oxen of Geryon* . . . . . . . . . oxen captured; Geryon, three-headed monster, killed.

*The Golden Apples of the Hesperides* . . . . . . . . . apples picked; Ladon, serpent guard, slain.

*Cerberus.* . . . . . . . . . . guard dog of the Underworld, grabbed by the throat and retrieved.

THIRTY-TWO TEETH

*Composition of normal adult dentition:*

Four canines—Eight incisors—Twelve molars—Eight pre-molars.

# HOW TO FOLD A BROADSHEET NEWSPAPER
## FOR EASY READING

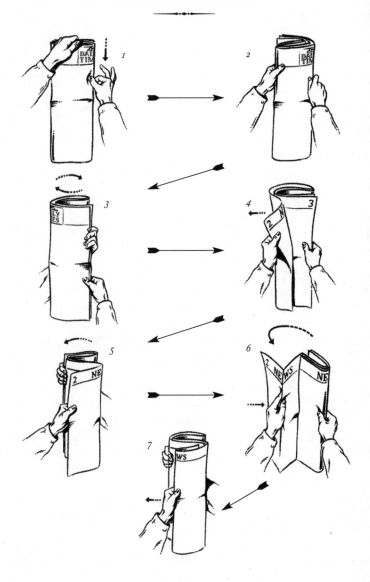

*Voyagers 1 and 2, interplanetary probes launched in August–September 1977, featured a phonograph record containing sounds and images representing life on Earth in case of their discovery by extraterrestrials. The contents of the 12-inch gold-plated copper disc, recorded in analogue format and encased in an aluminium jacket, were selected for the National Aeronautics and Space Administration by a committee chaired by Cornell University's Carl Sagan. There were printed messages from American president Jimmy Carter and United Nations Secretary-General Kurt Waldheim, and spoken greetings from Earth-people in fifty-five languages, beginning with Akkadian, spoken in Sumer about 6000 years ago, and ending with Wu, a modern Chinese dialect. Then, following a section on the sounds of Earth, was the following ninety minutes of music:*

Bach, Brandenburg Concerto No. 2 in F. First Movement, Munich Bach Orchestra, Karl Richter, conductor, 4:40. Java, court gamelan, 'Kinds of Flowers', recorded by Robert Brown, 4:43. Senegal, percussion, recorded by Charles Duvelle, 2:08. Zaire, Pygmy girls' initiation song, recorded by Colin Turnbull, 0:56. Australia, Aboriginal songs, 'Morning Star' and 'Devil Bird', recorded by Sandra LeBrun Holmes, 1:26. Mexico, 'El Cascabel', performed by Lorenzo Barcelata and the Mariachi México, 3:14. 'Johnny B. Goode', written and performed by Chuck Berry, 2:38. New Guinea, men's house song, recorded by Robert MacLennan, 1:20. Japan, shakuhachi, 'Tsuru no Sugomori' ('Crane's Nest') performed by Goro Yamaguchi, 4:51. Bach, 'Gavotte en rondeaux' from the Partita No. 3 in E major for violin, performed by Arthur Grumiaux, 2:55. Mozart, *The Magic Flute*, Queen of the Night aria, no. 14. Edda Moser, soprano. Bavarian State Opera, Munich, Wolfgang Sawallisch, conductor, 2:55. Georgian S.S.R., chorus, 'Tchakrulo', recorded by Radio Moscow, 2:18. Peru, panpipes and drum, recorded by Casa de la Cultura, Lima, 0:52. 'Melancholy Blues', performed by Louis Armstrong and his Hot Seven, 3:05. Azerbaijan S.S.R., bagpipes, recorded by Radio Moscow, 2:30. Stravinsky, *Rite of Spring*, Sacrificial Dance, Columbia Symphony Orchestra, Igor Stravinsky, conductor, 4:35. Bach, *The Well-Tempered*

*Clavier*, Book 2, Prelude and Fugue in C, No. 1. Glenn Gould, piano, 4:48. Beethoven, Fifth Symphony, First Movement, the Philharmonia Orchestra, Otto Klemperer, conductor, 7:20. Bulgaria, 'Izlel je Delyo Hagdutin', sung by Valya Balkanska, 4:59. Navajo Indians, Night Chant, recorded by Willard Rhodes, 0:57. Holborne, Paueans, Galliards, Almains and Other Short Aeirs, 'The Fairie Round', performed by David Munrow and the Early Music Consort of London, 1:17. Solomon Islands, panpipes, collected by the Solomon Islands Broadcasting Service, 1:12. Peru, wedding song, recorded by John Cohen, 0:38. China, ch'in, 'Flowing Streams', performed by Kuan P'ing-hu, 7:37. India, raga, 'Jaat Kahan Ho', sung by Surshri Kesar Bai Kerkar, 3:30. 'Dark Was the Night', written and performed by Blind Willie Johnson, 3:15. Beethoven, String Quartet No. 13 in B flat, Op. 130, Cavatina, performed by Budapest String Quartet, 6:37.

## NATIONAL COLOURS AND PLANTS

Green and gold, first worn by an Australian cricket team in 1899, were finally proclaimed our national colours in April 1984. This is despite the fact that the country's flag is red, white and blue, and its current coat of arms blue and gold.

The golden wattle, *Acacia pycnantha*, was proclaimed the official national floral emblem in August 1988, having been on the Coat of Arms since 1912. Since 1992, 1 September has been National Wattle Day. Other floral symbols are: Royal Bluebell (Australian Capital Territory); Waratah (New South Wales); Sturt's Desert Rose (Northern Territory); Cooktown Orchid (Queensland); Sturt's Desert Pea (South Australia); Tasmanian Blue Gum (Tasmania); Common Heath (Victoria); Red and Green Kangaroo Paw (Western Australia).

## FIVE RIVERS OF THE UNDERWORLD

Acheron—Styx—Phlegethon—Cocytus—Lethe

*Asia* (44,579,000 sq km)—*Africa* (30,065,000 sq km)—*North America* (24,256,000 sq km)—*South America* (17,819,000 sq km)—*Antarctica* (13,209,000 sq km)—*Europe* (9,938,000 sq km)—*Australia/Oceania* (7,687,000 sq km).

FOUNDATION DATES FOR WORLD AIRLINES

*Aer Lingus* (Ireland) 1936; *Aeroflot* (Russia) 1928[1]; *Aerolineas Argentinas* (Argentina) 1949; *Aeromexico* (Mexico) 1934[2]; *Air Canada* (Canada) 1937[3]; *Air France* (France) 1933; *Air India* (India) 1948; *Air New Zealand* (New Zealand) 1940[4]; *Alitalia* (Italy) 1940; *American Airlines* (USA) 1934; *British Airways* (UK) 1939[5]; *Cathay Pacific* (Hong Kong) 1946; *China Airlines* (China) 1959; *Delta* (USA) 1925[6]; *El Al* (Israel) 1948; *Garuda* (Indonesia) 1950[7]; *JAL* (Japan) 1951; *KLM-Royal Dutch* (Netherlands) 1919; *Lufthansa* (Germany) 1926; *MAS* (Malaysia) 1971; *Olympic Airways* (Greece) 1957; *Philippine Airlines* (Philippines) 1945; *Qantas* (Australia) 1920[8]; *Singapore Airlines* (Singapore) 1972; *Southwest Airlines* (US) 1945; *Thai Airways International* (Thailand) 1959; *United Airlines* (US) 1930; *Varig* (Brazil) 1927.

---

1 Formed as *Dobroflot* in the first Five-Year Plan, reorganised in 1932; 2 Formed as *Aeronaves de Mexico*, renamed in 1972; 3 Formed as *Trans-Canada Airlines*, renamed in 1964; 4 Formed as *Tasman Empire Airways*, renamed in 1965; 5 Formed as *British Overseas Airways Corporation; British European Airways* (BEA) formed in 1946; single entity, *British Airways*, created in 1975; 6 Originally a crop-duster, began carrying passengers 1929; 7 Originally part of *KLM*; 8 Formed as *Queensland and Northern Territory Aerial Services*.

*The Ayrshire Poet* Robert Burns; *The Bambino* Babe Ruth; *The Bard of Avon* William Shakespeare; *The Bearded Wonder* Bill Frindall; *The Beaver* Lord Beaverbrook; *The Brown Bomber* Joe Louis; *The Chairman of the Board* Frank Sinatra; *The Croucher* Gilbert Jessop; *The Dirty Dean* Rev William Corbet de Breton[1]; *The Dirty Digger* Rupert Murdoch; *The Don* Sir Donald Bradman; *The Dynamic Duo* Batman and Robin; *The Eagle* Eddie Edwards; *The English Virtuvius* Inigo Jones; *The First Grave Digger* Alexander Woollcott; *The Flying Doormat* Bruce Doull; *The Galloping Gasometer* Mick Nolan; *The Golden Bear* Jack Nicklaus; *The Grand Old Man* William Gladstone; *The Great Beast* Aleister Crowley; *The Great Cham* Dr Samuel Johnson; *The Greatest* Muhammad Ali; *The Hero of a Hundred Fights/The Iron Duke* The Duke of Wellington; *The Invincibles* 1948 Australian cricket team; *The King of the Sweep* Denis Compton; *The Last of the Mohicans* Hawkeye; *The Lithgow Flash* Marjorie Jackson; *The Mad Monk* Rasputin; *The Moody Dane* Hamlet; *The Prime Minister of Mirth* George Robey; *The Princess of Parallelograms* Lady Anna Millbanke[2]; *The Red Devils* Manchester United FC; *The Scottish Play* Macbeth; *The Shinboners* North Melbourne Football Club; *The Tichborne Claimant* Tom Castro.

1 Father of Lilli Langtry; 2 Bestowed by her husband, Lord Byron.

IDIOTS, MORONS, IMBECILES, CRETINS

According to British legal statute, an *idiot* is an individual with an IQ of less than 20, an *imbecile* has an IQ of between 20 and 49, and a *moron* an IQ between 50 and 69. *Cretins* are specifically persons with a deformity or mental retardation caused by a thyroid deficiency; cretinism is now more commonly called hyperthyroidism. Idiot is derived from the Greek for 'private person' (as in idiosyncracy); moron is from the Greek for 'foolish'; imbecile is a construction from a Latin phrase meaning 'without a stick'; cretin comes, via the French, from the word 'Christian', and implies a holy person—'God's fool', as it were.

*Argumentum ad antiquitatem*
Fallacy of asserting that something is right because it is old.

*Argumentum ad baculum*
Fallacy of threatening force to prevail in debate.

*Argumentum ad crumenam*
Fallacy that those with more money are more likely to be right.

*Argumentum ad hominem*
Fallacy of attacking the arguer rather than their argument.

*Argumentum ad ignorantiam*
Fallacy that something must be true because it has not been proven false, or false because it has not been proven true.

*Argumentum ad lazarum*
Fallacy of assuming that those with less money are more likely to be right.

*Argumentum ad logicam*
Fallacy of arguing that a proposition is false because it has been presented as the conclusion of a fallacious argument (right answers may be obtained by wrong methods).

*Argumentum ad misericordiam*
Fallacy of appealing to pity, also known as *special pleading*.

*Argumentum ad nauseam*
Fallacy that something is more likely to be true the more often it is heard.

*Argumentum ad novitatem*
Fallacy that something is right because it is new.

*Argumentum ad numerum*
Fallacy that the more people believe in a proposition, the likelier it is to be true.

*Argumentum ad populum*
Fallacy of 'appealing to the gallery'.

*Argumentum ad verecundiam*
Fallacy of 'appeal to authority', invoking the example of a famous person to win support.

*Bifurcation*
Fallacy of presenting a situation as having only two alternatives.

*Circulus in demonstrando*
Fallacy of assuming as a premise the conclusion which you wish to reach.

*Cum hoc ergo propter hoc*
Fallacy of asserting that events occuring simultaneously must be causally related.

*Natural Law fallacy*
Fallacy of appealing to nature, drawing an analogy between a conclusion and some aspect of natural world.

*Non sequitur*
Fallacy of drawing conclusion from unconnected premises.

*Petitio principii*
Fallacy of begging the question, occurring when premises of an argument implicitly assume the result.

*Plurium interrogationum*
Fallacy of demanding a simplistic answer to a complex question.

*Post hoc ergo propter hoc*
Fallacy of assuming that events happening sequentially must be causally related.

*Slippery slope fallacy*
Fallacy that one event will inevitably lead to harmful consequences.

*Straw man fallacy*
Fallacy of misrepresenting opponent's argument in order that one might better repudiate it.

*Tu quoque*
Fallacy of 'you too', that an action is acceptable because your opponent has performed it.

*Melvil Dewey (1851–1931) devised his system of classification while working as a twenty-one-year-old student assistant in the Amherst College library. He later founded the first library school at Columbia in January 1887.*

| | |
|---|---|
| 000–099 General works | 500–599 Pure science |
| 100–199 Philosophy | 600–699 Technology |
| 200–299 Religion | 700–799 Arts |
| 300–399 Social Sciences | 800–899 Literature |
| 400–499 Language | 900–999 Geography, history |

070.5028 Desktop publishing; 133.422 Satanism; 242 Meditations; 326 Slavery and emancipation; 480 Hellenic languages; 551.6 Greenhouse Effect; 616.89 Abnormal psychology; 635.976 Shrubs; 796.358 Cricket; 894 Ural-Altaic, Paleosiberian, Dravidian; 917.304 Directories to Campgrounds; 940.53493 Frank, Ann.

## FIVE KEY TEXTS OF THE OCCULT

*The Book of the Dead*, c. 1500 B.C.
A collection of Egyptian invocations and spells.

*Malleus Mallificorum* (*The Hammer of the Witches*), 1486
A handbook for the persecution of witches, written by two Dominican monks, Heinrich Kramer and James Sprenger.

*The Golden Asses*, 1566
Lucius Apuleius' tale of magical transformation, translated from Latin by William Adlington.

*The True and Faithful Relation of what passed between Doctor John Dee and some spirits*, 1659
Communications with the spirit world in Enochian.

*The Dogma and Ritual of Transcendent Magic*, 1856
Eliphas Levi's most important work.

*Aegir*    God of the sea.

*Balder*    God of innocence and light, son of Odin, twin brother of Hodur.

*Bragi*    God of poetry and music, son of Odin, wife of Idun.

*Forseti*    God of justice, son of Balder.

*Frey*    God of the fairyland, leader of the Vanir fertility gods.

*Freya*    Personification of the earth, sister of Frey, leader of the Vanir fertility goddesses.

*Frigga*    Odin's wife, Balder's mother.

*Heimdall*    Guard of Bifrost, the rainbow bridge.

*Hermod*    Son of Odin who traveled to Hel, land of the dead, in attempt to retrieve brother Balder.

*Hodur*    God of darkness, son of Odin, twin brother of Balder, who killed him with a mistletoe arrow given by Loki.

*Idun*    Personification of spring and youth.

*Loki*    God associated with mischief and misbehaviour.

*Niord*    God of summer.

*Odin*    Holiest of Norse gods, husband of Frigga, father of Balder, Hermod, Hodur, Thor, Vali and Vidar.

*Ran*    Aegir's wife, reputed to lure ships to their doom.

*Sif*    Thor's wife, whose exquisite hair was cut off by Loki.

*Skadi*    Goddess of winter.

*Sleipnir*    Odin's eight-footed war horse.

*Thor*    God of the sky and thunder, son and lieutenant to father Odin.

*Tyr*    God of war.

*Uller*    God of winter.

*Vali*    Son of Odin, groomed to wreak revenge on Loki.

*Vidar*    Son of Odin, who will live to revenge him after the apocalyptic battle between Gods and giants: Ragnarok.

'The Age of Television' . . . . . . . . . . . . . . . . . . . . . . Rob Swift, 1998
'Bad Television' . . . . . . . . . . . . . . . . . . . Boom Crash Opera, 2000
'Bad TV' . . . . . . . . . . . . . . . . . . . . . . . . . . . . . . Pink Lincolns, 1995
'Bio-TV' . . . . . . . . . . . . . . . . . . . . . . . . . . . . . . . . . . . Voivod, 1995
'Girl on TV' . . . . . . . . . . . . . . . . . . . . . . . . . . . . . . . . . LFO, 1999
'My TV' . . . . . . . . . . . . . . . . . . . . . . . . . . . . . . . . . . . . Vinx, 1991
'OK For TV' . . . . . . . . . . . . . . . . . . . . . . . . . . . . . Judy Lynn, 1993
'On My TV' . . . . . . . . . . . . . . . . . . . . . . . . . . Kat Eggleston, 1993
'On TV' . . . . . . . . . . . . . . . . . . . . . . . . . . . . . The Buggles, 1982
'Sad TV' . . . . . . . . . . . . . . . . . . . . . . . . . . . . . . The Visitors, 1979
'Television Addict' . . . . . . . . . . . . . . . . . . . . . Hoodoo Gurus, 1978
'Television Light' . . . . . . . . . . . . . . . . . . . Marshall Crenshaw, 1999
'Television Man' . . . . . . . . . . . . . . . . . . . . . . . Talking Heads, 1985
'Television Party' . . . . . . . . . . . . . . . . . . . . The Collins Kids, 1989
'Television Prison' . . . . . . . . . . . . . . . . . . . . . Robert Pollard, 1999
'Television Romeo' . . . . . . . . . . . . . . . . . . . The Depressions, 1978
'Television Screen' . . . . . . . . . . . . . . . . Radiators from Space, 1977
'Television Show' . . . . . . . . . . . . . . . . . . . . . Gravity Willing, 2001
'Television View' . . . . . . . . . . . . . . . . . . . . . . . The Vacants, 1978
'Television Vision' . . . . . . . . . . . . . . . . . . . . . . . The Fumes, 1994
'TV Ass' . . . . . . . . . . . . . . . . . . . . . . . . . . . . . The Skreppers, 2002
'TV Baby' . . . . . . . . . . . . . . . . . . . . . . . . . . . . . . Magazine, 1980
'TV Eye' . . . . . . . . . . . . . . . . . . . . . . . . . . . . . The Stooges, 1970
'TV Glue' . . . . . . . . . . . . . . . . . . . . . . . . . . . . . . . . . . . . X, 1985
'TV Mama' . . . . . . . . . . . . . . . . . . . . . . . . . . Big Joe Turner, 1951
'TV Man' . . . . . . . . . . . . . . . . . . . . . . . . . . . . . . . . Bolshoi, 1987
'TV Party' . . . . . . . . . . . . . . . . . . . . . . . . . . . . . Black Flag, 1979
'TV Set' . . . . . . . . . . . . . . . . . . . . . . . . . . . . . The Cramps, 1980
'TV Show' . . . . . . . . . . . . . . . . . . . . . . . . . . . . Dude of Life, 1994
'TV Song' . . . . . . . . . . . . . . . . . . . . . . . . . . . Glenn Branca, 1978

*This method is recommended by the New South Wales Oyster Foundation. A knife, oysters, and gloves if you are inexperienced, are all you need.*

1  Note where the hinge is.
2  Rest oyster on a sturdy surface, flat side up, hold firmly, push knife through top shell opposite hinge end.
3  Press downward on the knife, levering top shell up. Separate top and bottom shells completely, then rinse them.
4  Insert knife under oyster, cut adductor muscle.
5  Lift oyster out of flat shell, place on the other half.
6  The smooth side of the oyster presents a more attractive appearance than the bearded side. (All opened oysters are turned over by hand before being sold.)


## MILES FRANKLIN AWARD

| 1957 | Patrick White | *Voss* |
| 1958 | Randolph Stow | *To the Islands* |
| 1959 | Vance Palmer | *The Big Fellow* |
| 1960 | Elizabeth O'Connor | *The Irishman* |
| 1961 | Patrick White | *Riders in the Chariot* |
| 1962 | Thea Astley | *The Well-Dressed Explorer* |
| | George Turner | *The Cupboard under the Stairs* |
| 1963 | Sumner Locke Elliott | *Careful He Might Hear You* |
| 1964 | George Johnston | *My Brother Jack* |
| 1965 | Thea Astley | *The Slow Natives* |
| 1966 | Peter Mathers | *Trap* |
| 1967 | Thomas Keneally | *Bring Larks and Heroes* |
| 1968 | Thomas Keneally | *Three Cheers for the Paraclete* |
| 1969 | George Johnston | *Clean Straw for Nothing* |
| 1970 | Dal Stivens | *A Horse of Air* |
| 1971 | David Ireland | *The Unknown Industrial Prisoner* |

| 1972 | Thea Astley | *The Acolyte* |
| 1973 | No award | |
| 1974 | Ronald McKie | *The Mango Tree* |
| 1975 | Xavier Herbert | *Poor Fellow My Country* |
| 1976 | David Ireland | *The Glass Canoe* |
| 1977 | Ruth Park | *Swords and Crowns and Rings* |
| 1978 | Jessica Anderson | *Tirra Lirra by the River* |
| 1979 | David Ireland | *A Woman of the Future* |
| 1980 | Jessica Anderson | *The Impersonators* |
| 1981 | Peter Carey | *Bliss* |
| 1982 | Rodney Hall | *Just Relations* |
| 1983 | No award | |
| 1984 | Tim Winton | *Shallows* |
| 1985 | Christopher Koch | *The Doubleman* |
| 1986 | Elizabeth Jolley | *The Well* |
| 1987 | Glenda Adams | *Dancing on Coral* |
| 1988 | Date of award changed from year of publication to year of announcement | |
| 1989 | Peter Carey | *Oscar and Lucinda* |
| 1990 | Tom Flood | *Oceana Fine* |
| 1991 | David Malouf | *The Great World* |
| 1992 | Tim Winton | *Cloudstreet* |
| 1993 | Alex Miller | *The Ancestor Game* |
| 1994 | Rodney Hall | *The Grisly Wife* |
| 1995 | Helen Darville/ Demidenko | *The Hand That Signed the Paper* |
| 1996 | Christopher Koch | *Highways to a War* |
| 1997 | David Foster | *The Glade within the Grove* |
| 1998 | Peter Carey | *Jack Maggs* |
| 1999 | Murray Bail | *Eucalyptus* |
| 2000 | Kim Scott | *Benang* |
| | Thea Astley | *Drylands* |
| 2001 | Frank Moorhouse | *Dark Palaces* |
| 2002 | Tim Winton | *Dirt Music* |
| 2003 | Alex Miller | *Journey to the Stone Country* |

*Si bene te tua laus taxat sua laute tenebis*
If you are considered praiseworthy, you, elegant man, will keep your own property.

*Et necat eger amor non Roma rege tacente,*
*Roma reges una non anus eger amor*
And sick love kills, not from Rome, while the king is silent,
Rome, you will rule together, an old woman is not your sick love.

*Si nummi immunis*
Give me my fee, and I'll warrant you free. (Popular among Roman lawyers.)

*Ablata at alba*
Retired but pure.

## SAID OF WOLFGANG AMADEUS MOZART

'Your countenance…was so grave that many intelligent persons, seeing your talent so early developed and your face always serious and thoughtful, were concerned for the length of your life.'

> *Leopold Mozart, in a letter to his son Wolfgang.*

'He was always strumming on something—his hat, his watch fob, the table, the chair, as if they were the keyboard.'

> *Constanze Mozart, wife.*

'This boy will consign us all to oblivion!'

> *Johann Hasse after hearing* Ascanio in Alba, *Milan, 1771.*

'Too easy for children; too difficult for masters.'

> *Pianist and composer Artur Schnabel of Mozart's sonatas.*

'A spiritual creation, in which the details as well as the whole are pervaded by one spirit and by the breath of one life.'

> *Goethe on Mozart's operas.*

Can I get you a drink?
*Seez-eh beer itchkee ala beeleer meeyim?*

I'd love to have some company.
*Beeree-nin arkadashler-erndan chok memnoon oloorum.*

What's so funny?
*Komeek olan neh-deer.*

Is my Turkish that bad?
*Tewrk-chem oh kaddar kurtew mew?*

Shall we go somewhere quieter?
*Dah-ha sakeen beer yair-eh geedeleem mee.*

Would you like to come home with me?
*Beneem-leh eveh gelmek istair miseeniz?*

I'm not ready for that.
*Boonah hazzer day-eelim.*

Leave me alone please!
*Benee yalnerz berakern lewt-fen!*

I'm afraid we have to leave now.
*Korkarerm shimdee geetme-miz gerek.*

Thanks for the evening.
*Geh-jeh itchin teshek-kewr-lair.*

It was great.
*Chok gewzel-dee.*

THREE MUSKETEERS

Porthos—Aramis—Athos—(D'Artagnan)

Studied and named by the English psychiatrist John Todd (1914–1987), this psychopathological syndrome leads patients to feel that their bodies have altered in shape and size, the sensation often coinciding with hallucination and migraine, loss of a sense of time and a feeling of levitation. The condition honours *Alice's Adventures in Wonderland* (1865), the fictional creation of Lewis Carroll (Rev. Charles Dodgson), himself a lifelong martyr to migraines. Todd identified the complaint in 1955, as he began a distinguished twenty-four-year tenure as consultant psychiatrist at High Royds Hospital in Menston, West Yorkshire. He revealed in his career an unusual affinity for literature, composing medical studies of the Brontes and Anton Chekhov, and delineating psychiatric conditions he called the Othello and Big Brother syndromes.

## G s

G2    US, Japan.

G5    US, Japan, Germany, UK, France.

G7    US, Japan, Germany, UK, France, Canada, Italy.

G8    US, Japan, Germany, UK, France, Canada, Italy, Russia.

G10   US, Japan, Germany, UK, France, Canada, Belgium, Italy, Netherlands, Sweden, Switzerland. (Ten refers to those countries that are members of the International Monetary Fund.)

G15   Algeria, Argentina, Brazil, Chile, Egypt, India, Indonesia, Jamaica, Kenya, Malaysia, Mexico, Nigeria, Peru, Senegal, Sri Lanka, Venezuela, Zimbabwe. (Membership now 17.)

G20   US, Japan, Germany, UK, France, Canada, Italy, Indonesia, Argentina, Australia, Brazil, China, India, Mexico, Russia, Saudi Arabia, South Africa, South Korea and Turkey. (Nineteen members only.)

*M: For use by males; F: For use by females*

Don't cry.
*Nakanai-de.*

It's gonna be OK.
*Heiki-dayo.*

You don't love me anymore, do you?
F: *Mo watashi-no-koto aishitenai-none?*
M: *Mo boku-no-koto aishi-tenain-dane?*

Please tell me. I want to know.
F: *Doka ohiete. Shiritai-no.*
M: *Doka oshiete. Shiritain-da.*

I don't love you anymore.
*Mo aishitenai.*

I like you but I don't love you.
*Suki-dakedo aishitenai.*

I really don't love you anymore, so I'm going to change my phone number.
*Mo aishitenai-kara, denwa bango kaeru.*

Explain to me why!
F: *Setsumei shite!*
M: *Setsumei shite-kure!*

I made a mistake.
*Machigaeta.*

Thanks for the beautiful memories.
*Suteki-na omoide-o arigato.*

Don't be persistent.
F: *Shitsukoku shinai-de.*
M: *Shitsukoku suruna-you.*

In secret communiqués during World War II, British prime minister Winston Churchill was referred to variously as: Former Naval Person, Air Commodore Frankland, John Martin, Mr P., Naval Person, Colonel Warden.

## BLANKETING A STRETCHER

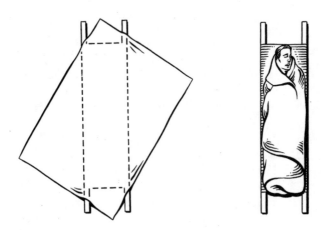

## SOME SYSTEMS OF VINE TRAINING, VITICULTURE

Alberate—Arched cane—Ballerina—Cassone padavano—
Cazenave— Cruzeta—Duplex—Flachbogen—Halbbogen—Hudson
River umbrella —Lincoln canopy—Palmette—Pendelbogen—
Pyramid—Raggi Bellussi —Smart-Dyson Trellis—Tatura
Trellis—Three-wire trellis—T trellis —Umbrella Kniffin—Y

| | |
|---|---|
| Henry Sewell | 7 May–20 May 1856 |
| William Fox | 20 May 1856–2 June 1856 |
| Edward Stafford | 2 June 1856–12 July 1861 |
| William Fox | 12 July 1861–6 August 1862 |
| Alfred Domett | 6 August 1862–30 October 1863 |
| Frederick Whitaker | 30 October 1863–24 November 1864 |
| Frederick Weld | 24 November 1864–16 October 1865 |
| Edward Stafford | 16 October 1865–28 June 1869 |
| William Fox | 28 June 1869–10 September 1872 |
| Edward Stafford | 10 September–11 October 1872 |
| George Waterhouse | 11 October 1872–3 March 1873 |
| William Fox | 3 March–8 April 1873 |
| Julius Vogel | 8 April 1873–6 July 1875 |
| Daniel Pollen | 6 July 1875–15 February 1876 |
| Sir Julius Vogel | 15 February–1 September 1876 |
| Harry Atkinson | 1 September 1876–13 October 1877 |
| Sir George Grey | 15 October 1877–8 October 1879 |
| John Hall | 8 October 1879–21 April 1882 |
| Frederick Whitaker | 21 April 1882–25 September 1883 |
| Harry Atkinson | 25 September 1883–16 August 1884 |
| Robert Stout | 16 August–28 August 1884 |
| Harry Atkinson | 28 August–3 September 1884 |
| Sir Robert Stout | 3 September 1884–8 October 1887 |
| Sir Harry Atkinson | 8 October 1887–24 January 1891 |
| John Balance | 24 January 1891–27 April 1893 |
| Richard Seddon | 1 May 1893–10 June 1906 |
| William Hall-Jones | 21 June–6 August 1906 |
| Sir Joseph Ward | 6 August 1906–28 March 1912 |
| Thomas Mackenzie | 28 March–10 July 1912 |
| William Massey | 10 July 1912–10 May 1925 |
| Sir Francis Bell | 14 May–30 May 1925 |
| Joseph Coates | 30 May 1925–10 December 1928 |
| Sir Joseph Ward | 10 December 1928–28 May 1930 |
| Sir George Forbes | 28 May 1930–6 December 1935 |

Michael Savage    6 December 1935–1 April 1940

Peter Fraser    1 April 1940–13 December 1949

Sir Sydney Holland    13 December 1949–20 September 1957

Keith Holyoake    20 September–12 December 1957

Walter Nash    12 December 1957–12 December 1960

Sir Keith Holyoake    12 December 1960–7 February 1972

John Marshall    7 February–8 December 1972

Norman Kirk    8 December 1972–31 August 1974

Wallace Rowling    6 September 1974–12 December 1975

Sir Robert Muldoon    12 December 1975–14 July 1984

David Lange    14 July 1984–8 August 1989

Geoffrey Palmer    8 August 1989–4 September 1990

Michael Moore    4 September–2 November 1990

James Bolger    2 November 1990–8 December 1997

Jennifer Shipley    8 December 1997–10 December 1999

Helen Clark    10 December 1999–

## STAGES IN A BULLFIGHT

| | |
|---|---|
| EL PASELLO/PASEO | Parade of the participants of the bullfight, sans bull. |
| TOREO DE CAPA | The peones/capeadores, assistants on foot, taunt the bull with their capes, giving the matador a chance to study the animal. The matador then tests the temperament of his quarry. |
| EL TERCIO DE VARAS | The picadores, mounted assistants, on horses both padded and blindfolded, thrust lances into the bull. |
| EL TERCIO DE BANDERILLAS | The banderillos thrust three pairs of brightly coloured dart sticks (banderillas) into the bull's neck and back. |
| EL TERCIO DE MULETA | Bullfighter shows his skill with the muleta (cape) and the sword. |
| LA ESTOCADA | The killing of the bull. The mulillas then drag the carcass from the ring. |

| | | | | | |
|---|---|---|---|---|---|
| I | 1 | VIII | 8 | LX | 60 |
| II | 2 | IX | 9 | LXX | 70 |
| III | 3 | X | 10 | LXXX | 80 |
| IV | 4 | XX | 20 | XC | 90 |
| V | 5 | XXX | 30 | C | 100 |
| VI | 6 | XL | 40 | D | 500 |
| VII | 7 | L | 50 | M | 1000 |

## DECATHLON EVENTS

*First Day*: 100 metres—Long jump—Shot put—High jump—400 metres.

*Second Day*: 110 metres hurdles—Discus—Pole vault—Javelin—1500 metres.

## CAESAR SALAD

1 clove garlic; 6 anchovy fillets; 3 tablespoons Parmesan cheese; 1 egg; 3 tablespoons olive oil; 1 tablespoon wine vinegar; 4 slices bread, cut thin; 2 tablespoons butter; 2 heads romaine lettuce.

Mash garlic in a large wooden salad bowl, discard pulp, then add anchovy fillets and cheese and mash into smooth paste. Coddle egg for one minute, add to anchovy-cheese mixture and work smooth, blend oil and vinegar. Butter bread on both sides, cube it small and brown until crisp for croutons. Wash, dry and crisp romaine, break into bowl, add croutons and toss until dressing has suffused leaves. Serves 4–6.

Named for Tijuana restaurateur Caesar Cardini, who first mixed it in an emergency in 1924 after finding himself short of salad ingredients, this tasty dish was nominated 'the greatest recipe to originate from the Americas in fifty years' by the International Society of Epicures in Paris.

'All the Guys That Turn Me On Turn Me Down'. . . . . . . . . . . . . .
                Gene Plott, Harold Powell & Roni Stoneman

'Are You Drinkin With Me, Jesus?'. . . . . . . . . . . . . . . . . . . . . . .
      Mojo Nixon, Country Dick Montana, Peter & Louise Berryman

'Did I Shave My Legs for This?' . . . . . . . . . . . . . . . . Deana Carter

'Don't Come Home A-Drinkin' With Lovin' on Yo-mind' . . . . . . .
                               Loretta Lynn

'Drop Kick Me Jesus (through the Goal Posts of Life)'. . . . . . . . . .
                            Paul Charles Craft

'Get Your Biscuits in the Oven, and Your Buns in the Bed'. . . . . . .
               Kinky Friedman & the Texas Jewboys

'Here's a Quarter (Call Someone Who Cares)'. . . . . . . . Travis Tritt

'How Come Your Dog Don't Bite Nobody But Me?'. . . . Mel Tillis

'I Like Bananas Because They Have No Bones'. . . . . . Chris Yacich

'I Wish I Were a Lesbian' . . . . . . . . . . . . . Loudon Wainwright III

'I'm Just an Old Chunk of Coal (But I'm Gonna Be a Diamond
    Someday' . . . . . . . . . . . . . . . . . . . . . . . . . . . . . Billy Joe Shaver

'If I Had It to Do All over Again, I'd Do It All over You'. . . . . . . .
                        Dan Hicks and his Hot Licks

'If the Phone Doesn't Ring, It's Me' . . . . . . . . . . . . . Jimmy Buffett

'If You Can't Live Without Me, Why Aren't You Dead?'. . . . . . . . .
        Benjamin Costello, Alexis Feltham & Jason Whalley

'Jesus Loves Me But He Can't Stand You'. . . . . . . . . . . . . . . . . . . .
                         Austin Lounge Lizards

'My Wife Ran off With My Best Friend, and I Sure Do Miss Him'
                               Phil Earhart

'Pardon Me, I've Got Someone to Kill' . . . . . . . . . Johnny Paycheck

'She Broke My Heart, I Broke Her Jaw' . . . . . . . . . . . Rick Stanley

'Thank God and Greyhound She's Gone' . . . . . . . . . . . . Roy Clark

*Solution from p. 86: it is not possible.*

550 B.C. . . . . . . . . . . . . . . . . . . . . . . . . . . . . . . . . . . . . . . . . . . . . Kites
500 B.C. . . . . . . . . . . . . . . . . . . . . . . . . . . . . . . . . . . Magnifying lens
300 B.C. . . . . . . . . . . . . . . . . . . . . . . . . . . . . . . . . . . . Industrial drill
210 B.C. . . . . . . . . . . . . . . . . . . . . . . . . . . . . . . . . . Navigation canals
200 B.C. . . . . . . . . . . . . . . . . . . . . . . . . . . . . . . . . Organic pesticides
180 B.C. . . . . . . . . . . . . . . . . . . . . . . . . . . . . . . . . . . Magic lantern
50 B.C. . . . . . . . . . . . . . . . . . . . . . . . . . . . Paper; hot air balloons
A.D. 300 . . . . . . . . . . . . . . . . . . . . . . . . . . . Fireworks/gunpowder
A.D. 580 . . . . . . . . . . . . . . . . . . . . . . . . . . . . . . . . . . . . Toilet paper

## WEDDING TOASTS

*A formal wedding reception generally follows this pattern of toasts:*

1  The Loyal Toast (to the reigning monarch): proposed by master of ceremonies or the bride's father, without speech. Smoking is not usually permitted until the toast has been made.
2  Toast to the Bridal Couple: proposed by friend of bride's family after speech.
3  Toast to Bridesmaids: proposed by groom after response to the foregoing.
4  Toast to Groom: proposed by best man after response to foregoing.
5  Toast to Parents of Bride: proposed by relative or friend.
6  Response by Bride's father.
7  Toast to Parents of Groom: proposed by relative or friend.
8  Response by Groom's father.
9  Reading of telegrams by best man and groomsmen.

## SEVEN DWARFS

Bashful—Doc—Dopey—Grumpy—Happy—Sleepy—Sneezy

*'Enlightened souls who prefer dry wines to sweet, sense to sentiment, wit to humour, and clean English to slang.'* So did the American journalist Ambrose Bierce (1842–1914) identify the audience for his Devil's Dictionary, *published in 1911. Bierce had first tried his hand at satiric definitions in his columns in 1875; his selection of the best thousand has seldom been out of print since.*

*Australia,* n. A country lying in the South Sea whose industrial and commercial development has been unspeakably retarded by an unfortunate dispute as to whether it is a continent or an island.

*Belladonna,* n. In Italian a beautiful lady; in English a deadly poison. A striking example of the essential identity of the two tongues.

*Bore,* n. A person who talks when you wish him to listen.

*Corporation,* n. An ingenious device for obtaining individual profit without individual responsibility.

*Cui bono?* (Latin) What good would that do *me?*

*Diplomacy,* n. The patriotic art of lying for one's country.

*Erudition,* n. Dust shaken out of a book into an empty skull.

*Famous,* adj. Conspicuously miserable.

*Happiness,* n. An agreeable sensation arising from contemplating the misery of another.

*Historian,* n. A broad-gauge gossip.

*Immoral,* adj. Inexpedient.

*Impunity,* n. Wealth.

*Lawyer,* n. One skilled in circumvention of the law.

*Longevity,* n. Uncommon extension of the fear of death.

*Once,* adv. Enough.

*Peace,* n. In international affairs, a period of cheating between two periods of fighting.

*Rebel,* n. A proponent of a new misrule who has failed to establish it.

*Virtues,* n. pl. Certain abstentions.

*War,* n. A by-product of the arts of peace.

## UNUSUAL MEASURES

A cran . . . . . . . . . . . . . . . . . . . . 45 gallons (204.3L) of fresh herring
A firkin . . . . . . . . . . . . . . . . . . . . . . . 56 pounds (25.4kg) of butter
A frail . . . . . . . . . . . . . . . . . . . . . . . 50 pounds (22.7kg) of raisins
A clove . . . . . . . . . . . . . . . . . . . 8–10 pounds (3.63–4.54kg) of cheese


## SOME AVERAGE PH VALUES

PH stands for 'potential of hydrogen'. A solution is acidic when its pH is less than 7, alkaline when more. Most acidic is 1, most alkaline 14. The scale is logarithmic; that is, a solution with a pH of 3 is ten times as acidic as a solution with a pH of 4.

| | |
|---|---|
| 1.0 – 3.0 gastric juice | 5.0 black coffee |
| 1.6 lime juice | 5.8 potatoes |
| 2.3 lemon juice | 6.4 milk |
| 2.8 vinegar | 7.0 water |
| 3.0 apples (approximate) | 7.35 human blood |
| 3.3 strawberries | 8.2 seawater |
| 3.5 orange juice | 10.5 milk of magnesia |
| 4.2 tomatoes | 13.0 sodium hydroxide |


## FIVE PILLARS OF ISLAM

1 Witnessing that God is One and Mohammed is his prophet
2 Praying five times a day
3 Giving a portion of one's wealth to charity annually (Zakat)
4 Fasting during the daylight hours of Ramadan
5 Making the pilgrimage to Mecca at least once (Hajj)

John Sackville Richard Tufton (2nd Lord Hothfield), Kent, 1897–98.

Major-General Sir Harold Goodeve Ruggles-Brise, University of Oxford, 1883.

Commandur Rajagopalachari Rangachari, India, 1948–49.

HRH Prince Albert Ludwig Victor Ernest Anton Christian Victor of Schleswig-Holstein, I Zingari, 1887.

Ivo Francis Walter Bligh (8th Lord Darnley), Kent and England, 1877–83.

Lord Archibald Brabazon-Sparrow Acheson (4th Earl of Gosford), MCC, 1864.

HH Bhupendrasingh Rajindersingh (Maharajah of Patiala), India, 1911–36.

Seton Robert De La Poer Horsley Beresford, Middlesex, 1909.

Lord John Francis Granville Scrope Egerton Brackley (4th Earl of Ellesmere), MCC, 1898–1905.

HRH Rana Sahib Shri Natuarisinhji Bhavisinhji (Maharajah of Porbandar), India, 1932.

## ANAGRAMS FOR TEN AUSTRALIAN PRIME MINISTERS

|  |  |
|---|---|
| *Edmund Barton* | Rotund Bed Man |
| *Alfred Deakin* | Kneel'd Afraid |
| *Billy Hughes* | Bully, He Sigh |
| *John Curtin* | Churn Joint |
| *Ben Chifley* | Inch Feebly |
| *Sir Robert Menzies* | Breezier in Storms |
| *Gough Whitlam* | Whim Got Laugh |
| *Robert Hawke* | Wreath Broke |
| *Paul Keating* | Entail UK Gap |
| *John Winston Howard* | Soon John Withdrawn |

*British Army (WWI)*
Ack Beer Charlie Don Edward Freddie Gee Harry Ink Johnnie King London Emma Nuts Oranges Pip Queen Robert Esses Toc Uncle Vic William X-ray Yorker Zebra

*Royal Navy (WWI)*
Apples Butter Charlie Duff Edward Freddy George Harry Ink Johnny King London Monkey Nuts Orange Pudding Queenie Robert Sugar Tommy Uncle Vinegar Willie Xerxes Yellow Zebra

*Royal Air Force (1924–1942)*
Ace Beer Charlie Don Edward Freddie George Harry Ink Johnnie King London Monkey Nuts Orange Pip Queen Robert Sugar Toc Uncle Vic William X-Ray Yorker Zebra

*Joint US Army/Navy Alphabet (WWII)*
Able Baker Charlie Dog Easy Fox George How Item Jig King Love Mike Nan Oboe Peter Queen Roger Sail Tare Uncle Victor William X-Ray Yoke Zero

*NATO Alphabet (1956– )*
Alpha Bravo Charlie Delta Echo Foxtrot Golf Hotel India Juliet Kilo Lima Mike November Oscar Papa Quebec Romeo Sierra Tango Uniform Victor Whiskey X-Ray Yankee Zulu

    Originally adopted for use by members of the North Atlantic Treaty Organisation, the NATO Alphabet is the official phonetic code of the International Civil Aviation Organisation and the International Telegraphers Union.

## METABASIS

Paranthetic clarification inserted into a longer sentence. Thus St Paul in 1 Corinthians 13:1: 'And now abideth faith, hope, charity, these three; but the greatest of these is charity.'

*Rations for the Slaves*
For the actual labourers four pecks of wheat in the winter months, and four and a half in summer. The overseer, housekeeper, foreman and head-shepherd should receive three pecks. The chain-gang should receive four pounds of bread a day in winter, five from the time when they begin to dig the vines until the figs start to ripen, and then back to four again.

*Wine for the Slaves*
For three months after the harvest, they should drink rough wine. In the fourth month, half a pint a day, or about two gallons a month. For the fifth, sixth, seventh and eighth months, the ration should be a pint a day, or four gallons a month. For the remaining four months, give them one and a half pints a day, or six gallons a month. For the feasts of the Saturnalia and Compitalia (December) there should be an extra ration per man of two and a half gallons. The total wine issue per man for a year should be about forty-two gallons. An additional amount can be given as a bonus to the chain-gang, depending on how well they work. A reasonable quantity for them to have to drink per annum is about sixty gallons.

*Relish for the Slaves*
Keep all the windfall olives you can. Then keep the ripe olives from which only a small yield would be gained. Issue them sparingly to make them last as long as possible. When the olives are finished, give them fish-pickle and vinegar. Give each man a pint of oil a month. A peck of salt should be enough for a man for a year.

*Clothes for the Slaves*
A tunic three and a half feet long and a blanket-cloth every other year. When you issue a tunic or cloak, take in the old one to make rough clothes. You ought to give them a good pair of clogs every other year.

*from Cato's* Di Agri Cultura, 170 B.C.

| Sidekick | Detective | Creator |
|---|---|---|
| Asta* | Nick, Nora Charles | Dashiell Hammett |
| Bunter | Lord Peter Wimsey | Dorothy L. Sayers |
| Mike Burden | Inspector Wexford | Ruth Rendell |
| Paul Drake, Della Street | Perry Mason | Erle Stanley Gardiner |
| Inspectors Lucas, Lapointe, Janvier | Inspector Maigret | Georges Simenon |
| Captain Hastings | Hercule Poirot | Agatha Christie |
| Ted Jerningham, Toby Sinclair | 'Bulldog' Drummond | 'Sapper' aka Herman Cyril McNeile |
| Sergeant Lewis | Inspector Morse | Colin Dexter |
| Inspector Richard Queen | Ellery Queen | Manfred Lee/Frederic Dannay |
| Ratso | Kinky Friedman | Kinky Friedman |
| Squire Randolph | Uncle Abner | Melville Post |
| Tinker | Sexton Blake | Various |
| Velda | Mike Hammer | Mickey Spillane |

* The schnauzer in Hammett's *The Thin Man* (1934).

## TWENTY SONGS FEATURING PHILOSOPHERS IN THEIR TITLES

'Aquinas'. . . . . . . . . . . . . . . . . . . . . . . . . . . . . Ray Obiedo, 1995
'Berkeley Woman' . . . . . . . . . . . . . . . . . . . . . . . John Denver, 1973
'Berlin Blues'. . . . . . . . . . . . . . . . . . . . . Climax Blues Band, 1973
'Flight of Plato' . . . . . . . . . . . . . . . . . . . . . . Asphalt Jungle, 2002
'Hegel's Fantasy Guy' . . . . . . . . . . . Klucevsek & Alan Bern, 2001
'Hobbes Theme' . . . . . . . . . . . . . . . . Climax Golden Twins, 2001
'Jacques Derrida'. . . . . . . . . . . . . . . . . . . . . . . . Scritti Politi, 1982
'Lacan Woto Kumu'. . . . . . . . . . . . . . . . . Geoffrey Oryema, 1991
'Moore Shit'. . . . . . . . . . . . . . . . . . . . . . . . . . . . Luke Vibert, 1999
'Nailing Descartes to the Wall'. . . . . . . . . . . . . . Propagandhi, 1996
'Nietzsche with a Pizza' . . . . . . . . . . . . . . . . . . . . Skin Yard, 1991
'Nietzsche's Ass' . . . . . . . . . . . . . . . . . . . . . . . . Peter Green, 1998
'The Rape of Heidegger Geiger' . . . . . . . . . . . . Mr Swenson, 2000
'Saw Mill'. . . . . . . . . . . . . . . . . . . . . . . . . . . . . Miles Davis, 1990
'Socrates the Python' . . . . . . . . . . . . . . . . . . . Peter Murphy, 1985
'Transkription for Soren Kierkegaard' . . . . Cornelis Vreeswijk, 1976
'Wittgenstein Blues'. . . . . . . David Moss & Michael Rodach, 2000
'Wittgenstein Mon Amour' . . . . . . . . . . . . . . . . . Finisterre, 1999
'Working for de Man' . . . . . . . . . . . . . . . . . . . . Roy Orbison, 1962
'You, Kant, Stop the Music'. . . . . . . . . . . . . . Village People, 1981

## CHILDHOOD DISEASES

| Disease | Incubation Period | Fever Appears |
| --- | --- | --- |
| Chickenpox | 7–21 days | Slight |
| Rubella | 14–21 days | First two days |
| Measles | 7–14 days | First five days |
| Mumps | 14–28 days | First day |
| Pertussis (whooping cough) | 7–14 days | First seven days |

*Apes* Shrewdness
*Asses* Pace
*Badgers* Cete
*Bear* Sloth
*Cats* Clowder
*Coots* Covert
*Elks* Gang
*Foxes* Skulk
*Geese* Gaggle (on ground)/
Skein (in flight)
*Guinea Fowls* Confusion
*Hares* Husk

*Leopards* Leap
*Lions* Sault/Pride
*Moles* Labour
*Nightingales* Watch
*Owls* Parliament
*Partridges* Covey
*Quail* Bevy
*Snakes* Bed
*Starlings* Murmuration
*Toads* Knot
*Turtles* Bale
*Whales* Gam/Pod

## TESTING AN EGG'S FRESHNESS

*Place egg in pan of cold water. If it:*

1 Lies on its side, it's fresh
2 Tilts at an angle, it's about a week old
3 Stands straight up, it's about ten days old
4 Floats, it should be discarded.

## BURNS

*First-degree*: Affects outer layer of skin, causing pain, redness, swelling.
*Second-degree:* Affects outer and underlying layer of the skin, causing pain, redness, swelling, and blistering.
*Third-degree:* Extends into deeper tissues, causing brown or blackened skin that may be numb.

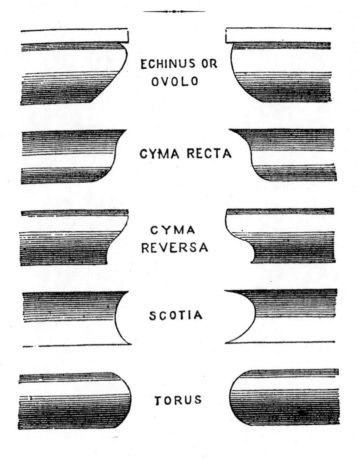

ECHINUS OR OVOLO

CYMA RECTA

CYMA REVERSA

SCOTIA

TORUS

WORKS OF JOSEPH HAYDN

365 accompaniments to Scottish songs, 163 pieces for baritone, 118 symphonies, 83 quartets, 44 piano sonatas, 39 canzonets, 24 concertos, 24 trios, 19 operas, 15 masses, 13 hymns, 12 German/Italian songs, 10 smaller church pieces, 5 oratorios.

The fast-food restaurant chain founded in 1955 by an honorary Kentucky colonel called Harland Sanders rose to prominence after its 1964 acquisition for $US2 million by flamboyant entrepreneur John Y. Brown. By the time it came under the control of the vodka giant Heublein in 1971, it was a $US250 million enterprise.

Originally known as Kentucky Fried Chicken, it adopted its current nomenclature in 1991. KFC was spun off by PepsiCo in October 1997 as part of Tricon Global Restaurants Inc, which also controls Pizza Hut and Taco Bell; TGR has recently been renamed Yum! Brands Inc.

| Item | Weight | Energy | Cholesterol |
|---|---|---|---|
| EC Chicken Drumstick | 60 grams (10g of fat) | 668kJ/160 calories (90 from fat) | 70mg |
| EC Chicken Thigh | 114 grams (26g of fat) | 1548kJ/370 calories (230 from fat) | 120mg |
| Hot & Spicy Drumstick | 60 grams (9g of fat) | 628kJ /150 calories (80 from fat) | 65mg |
| Hot & Spicy Thigh | 128 grams (28g of fat) | 1674kJ/400 calories (250 from fat) | 125mg |
| Zinger Sandwich with Sauce | 224 grams (41g of fat) | 2845kJ/680 calories (370 from fat) | 90mg |
| Crispy Strips | 151 grams (24g of fat) | 1674kJ/400 calories (220 from fat) | 75mg |
| Hot BBQ Wings | 157 grams (33g of fat) | 2259kJ/540 calories (300 from fat) | 150mg |

In Judaeo-Christian morality, the seven deadly sins are: anger, envy, gluttony, greed, lust, pride and sloth. Indian political and spiritual leader Mohandas Karamachand Gandhi (1869–1948) devised his own list of those traits most perilous to humanity:

1 Wealth without Work; 2 Pleasure without Conscience; 3 Science without Humanity; 4 Knowledge without Character; 5 Politics without Principle; 6 Commerce without Morality; 7 Worship without Sacrifice.

## ALPHABET MINUTE

In this popular Victorian parlour game, participants write a general topic of conversation and a letter of the alphabet on a slip of paper then place them in a hat. Players form pairs, one of whom, when their turn comes, picks a slip from said hat. The idea is to conduct a conversation on the topic in which each sentence commences with a letter of the alphabet, beginning with the letter on the paper. A timer keeps track of how quickly the pair return to their starting letter. Example:

Subject: *The Uncyclopedia*

Letter: A

Player 1: 'A remarkable work, *The Uncyclopedia*, don't you agree?'

Player 2: 'But who would want to read it?'

Player 1: 'Clever people who love knowledge for the sake of it.'

Player 2: 'Do you really think so?'

Player 1: 'Esoteric information is a source of delight for many readers.'

Player 2: 'Fine, but there are many books on the market like it.'

Player 1: 'Generally they have neither the breadth of information nor the delightful sense of fun.'

Player 2: 'Haigh is definitely one of the great minds of the century.'

Player 1: 'I wouldn't go that far.'

Player 2: 'Just thought I'd try to squeeze it in.'

'If a writer has friends connected with the press, it is the plain duty of those friends to do their utmost to help him. What matter if they exaggerate, or even lie? The simple sober truth has no chance whatever of being listened to, and it's only by volume of shouting that the ear of the public is held.'

George Gissing, *New Grub Street* (1891)

'The reviewer, jaded though he may be, is professionally interested in books, and out of the thousands that appear annually, there are probably fifty or a hundred he would enjoy writing about. If he is a top-notcher in his profession he may get hold of ten or twenty of them: more probably he gets hold of two or three. The rest of his work, however conscientious he may be in praising or damning, is in essence humbug. He is pouring his immortal soul down the drain, half a pint at a time.'

George Orwell, 'Confessions of a Book Reviewer' (1946)

'Listen, we've been having a bit of trouble with you book critics lately. It's not a very manly trade, is it? Quite frankly, your attempts to review books like this in the past have been absolutely pathetic...So we've had a word with the men at a sort of security firm in South London, and together we've come up with what we feel is a very reasonable offer. "Blackmail" is a dirty word. But it's accurate. We will give you money, in cash, for every decent review you come up with. That'll be ten quid for quite a good little notice, £15 for a thoroughly appreciative warm welcome for the book, and twenty pounds for a rave. On the other hand, we shall be forced to take reprisals if you start knocking it. This will mean, and please don't grumble that you haven't been warned, severe physical pain (or breakages) to parts of your body for a bad notice; severe cutting and bending of bits of your anatomy for a smart-arse notice; and I'm afraid that for an extremely bad notice you'd do better to leave the country. Well, there's your warning. Poor notices can cause a certain amount of bad blood. And in this case, it will be yours.'

Eric Idle, *Rutland Dirty Weekend Book* (1976)